Decision Debt

Decision Debt

The Real Bottleneck in Software Delivery

Rowan Gobey

Prestige Publishing Worldwide

Decision Debt: The Real Bottleneck in Software Delivery

First edition, 2026.
Published by Prestige Publishing Worldwide.

ISBN: 978-1-7647347-0-7

www.rowangobey.com

To Echo, Violet, and George —

who fill my life with colour.

Thank you for tolerating my antics.
Thank you more for encouraging them.
But most of all, thank you for being the reason
they mattered enough to write down.

Contents

Introduction

MOST software teams are broken in predictable ways.

The standup that's become a way of micromanaging each team member. The backlog with four hundred unrefined tickets, or worse, four hundred refined tickets, written two years ago by a product manager (PM) who's long gone. The product owner (PO) who can't make a decision without escalating. The retro that's been running the same five complaints for nine months which is "out of our hands" to resolve. The "blocker" column that's just where work goes to die.

The teams know they're broken. They've usually had a coach in already, or they've done a Scaled Agile Framework (SAFe) rollout, or they've reorganised twice. Sometimes all three. None of it stuck, because none of it touched the actual problem.

The actual problem is that decisions, not code, are the bottleneck.

That's the spine of this book. Everything in it follows from that one observation, and most of what's wrong with how teams talk about delivery follows from missing it.

Eliyahu Goldratt and Jeff Cox wrote *The Goal* in 1984 about a manufacturing plant. The book is a novel, technically — a plant manager called Alex Rogo gets ninety days to save his factory, meets a physicist on a plane, and figures out that the factory's output is governed by its slowest step. Everything else is either feeding that step or getting in its way. Find the constraint, exploit it, subordinate everything else to it. If you optimise anywhere else, you're just making the warehouse fuller while the bottleneck still produces at the same rate.

The book has aged extraordinarily well, and it's been applied to everything from hospitals to call centres to chip fabs. It applies to software too, but you have to be careful with the metaphor. Software isn't a production line. The unit of work is fuzzier than a finished bicycle. The constraint moves around — almost esoteric in nature — it can be a person one week and an environment the next. Anyone who's read *The Goal* and tried to treat story points as widgets per hour finds out fast that the analogy breaks if you push it too hard.

What does carry across is the thinking pattern. *Where is the work actually stuck?* That's the question. And in software, almost every time, the answer is: someone is waiting for someone else to decide something. The developer is waiting on a clarification. The pull request (PR) is waiting on a reviewer. The story is waiting for the PO to confirm an acceptance criterion. The release is waiting on a sign-off. The team is waiting for a direction.

It's almost never typing speed. It hasn't been typing speed for a long time. The teams that look fast aren't typing faster than the teams that look slow — they're deciding faster, deciding earlier, and deciding with less ceremony. Their bottleneck is somewhere else, or they've moved it somewhere they can live with.

Once you start looking through this lens, the dysfunctions rearrange themselves. The 400-ticket backlog isn't a refinement problem, it's a decision-deferral graveyard. The standup that runs forty minutes isn't a discipline problem, it's a sign that decisions made in the meeting are the only decisions getting made that day. The team that "can't estimate" isn't bad at estimating — they don't have enough information to decide anything, and the estimate is where that surfaces.

Most of what looks like complexity is decision debt.

And that debt has a cause. Organisations don't accumulate it by accident — they build it, one approval gate at a time, usually for reasons that made sense in isolation. A bad incident two years ago. A regulatory requirement. A senior person who needed to be kept in the loop. The cumulative effect is a system in which the smartest people in the building are no longer trusted to make decisions on their own, and after enough years they stop trusting themselves to make them. The architect waits for the chief technology officer (CTO). The senior developer waits for the architect. The PO escalates rather than deciding. Over time the team forgets it ever could decide, and every attempt to fix the slowness from above adds another approval gate to the system that caused it.

The other influence is the Toyota Production System (TPS) — the tradition behind lean. TPS gives the book something Goldratt doesn't: the operating principle that the people closest to the work usually know what's wrong with it, and the manager's job is to clear the obstacles that stop them fixing it themselves. That's where the book's bias toward light touch comes from, and toward asking rather than telling.

Slow delivery isn't a staff problem. It's a trust problem. We'll come back to that.

If decisions are the constraint, then the AI thing makes a lot more sense than the discourse around it suggests.

Teams have spent the last two years in various states of confusion about what AI tooling is doing to their delivery. Some teams got dramatically faster. Some teams got dramatically slower. Some report that they're shipping more code but somehow finishing less work. The narrative that's emerged is roughly: AI is complicated, the old playbook needs rewriting, everything is different now.

It isn't. AI didn't change the underlying problem. It exposed it. AI merely eliminated one bottleneck from the equation, making the real bottlenecks that much more obvious.

Code used to be expensive enough that fast typing covered for slow deciding. A developer who could chew through three tickets a day made the team look productive even if the tickets were ambiguous, the acceptance criteria were vague, and half the work would get reverted next sprint. The bottleneck was always upstream of the keyboard, but the keyboard was busy enough that it looked like the constraint.

Now the keyboard is essentially free. A developer with an AI coding tool open can produce a week's worth of last year's output in a morning. The keyboard is no longer the constraint, and it never was — but now the cover is gone. What you see, when you look at the team that's "struggling with AI," is almost always a team that was already struggling with decision throughput. They produce more code than ever, and finish less of it, because the new code is hitting the same review queues, the same PO ambiguity, the same approval chains, the same merge-conflict-of-the-week. It's water arriving faster at a dam that was already full.

The teams that thrived with AI tooling are the teams that already had decision throughput sorted. Their POs decide quickly. Their reviewers turn things around. Their definition of done is unambiguous enough that you know whether you're finished without asking. They didn't get faster *because* of AI. They were already fast, and AI removed the one constraint that was still slowing them down.

This isn't a "things were simpler before" book. Things were never simpler. They were just less visible.

This book is for delivery managers, scrum masters, agile coaches, engineering managers, and anyone else whose job nominally involves making a software team work better. Read it as the book you wish someone had handed you when you started doing this seriously, before you assumed the answer was somewhere in the SAFe materials or the Scrum Guide or the next coaching certification.

The answer isn't there. The answer is that almost every team you'll ever join is broken in roughly the same five ways, and there's a small set of cheap, observable, fast-acting fixes that work at almost every one of them. Not "build a culture of psychological safety." Not "embrace continuous improvement." Specific things. Walk the board right to left in your standup. Cap work in progress (WIP) at the column level. Make the PO answer the unanswered question before estimation, not after. Time-box the spike. Kill the recurring meeting that nobody can defend.

This is a practitioner's book, not a textbook. It has an opinion. It's not framework gospel — it doesn't matter whether you're running Scrum, Kanban, SAFe, ScrumBan, or some hybrid your

CTO invented in 2019 and named after a constellation. What matters is whether work is moving and whether decisions are being made. Frameworks are containers; the question is what's in them.

It's also not a coaching book. There are good coaching books out there. They tend to be long, soft, and unfalsifiable, and they take a year to know whether they worked. This one promises something different: pick up a chapter, apply it on Monday, see results by Friday. Every chapter has to clear that bar or it's not in the book. If you can't act on it within the week, it's the wrong chapter.

The other bar every chapter has to clear is light touch. The fixes in this book are the smallest moves that produce the largest changes. Not transformations. Not rebuilds. Not "culture journeys." If a fix needs you to restructure the org, hire three people, or run a six-month programme, it's the wrong fix. There's almost always a smaller version of it that works, and that smaller version is what the book is about. Pulling the right lever takes more observation than effort. The effort is in finding the lever, not in pulling it.

That promise drove a lot of the structure. Part 1 is the diagnosis: how to see the bottleneck, how to recognise the recurring patterns, why the chapter rescue works. Part 2 is the diagnostic toolkit — ceremonies, estimation, spikes, definitions of ready and done — but reframed as instruments for measuring decision throughput, not as "how to do scrum properly." Part 3 is the cheap fixes. Each chapter is a recurring dysfunction, with the rescue that works overnight. Part 4 is what's changed in the AI era and what hasn't.

You don't need to read the parts in order. The book is built so you can pick up the chapter that matches what's broken on your team this week, apply it, and come back for the next one when the next thing breaks. The early parts give you the lens; the later parts give you the levers. My promise to the reader is that this book will not contain anything but what is required, no extra padding to make the spine stick out more on your bookshelf — so apologies in advance if it's hard to find.

A note on what this book isn't going to do.

It's not going to give you a culture transformation programme. Cultures shift slowly, and they shift because behaviour shifts first. This book is about behaviour. The culture follows.

It's not going to defend any framework's honour. Scrum works and Scrum fails. Kanban works and Kanban fails. The framework was never the variable.

It's not going to be a book about how to control your team better. The opposite, mostly. Most of what's in here is about removing things — meetings, approval gates, ambiguous tickets, status reports that nobody reads — and resisting the instinct to fix problems by adding more process. The natural managerial response to a problem is to add: a new ceremony, a new template, a new check, a new sign-off. The book argues for subtracting first.

It's not going to be entertaining the way *The Phoenix Project* is entertaining. Gene Kim's novel about an IT department racing to save itself from shutdown — the most widely read delivery story in the industry — is a good one, but it stops where the playbook would start. Bill Palmer figures out what's wrong; the book doesn't tell you what to do on the Monday of week one when your team's standup is forty minutes of status-reporting to a manager. This book does.

And it's not going to pretend that delivery management is hard. Most of it isn't. Most of it is noticing the same five things and doing the same handful of cheap fixes, week after week, at company after company. The hard part is staying disciplined about it — not getting pulled into the framework debates, the org-chart restructures, the tooling migrations, the AI hype cycle, the next certification. Staying focused on where the work is actually stuck and unsticking it. With the lightest touch you can get away with.

That's the job. That's the book.

Let's get shit done.

Chapter 1: Seeing the System

YOU can't change a system you haven't seen.

This is the whole game in Part 1. Almost every mistake delivery managers make in their first month — whether it's their first month at a new company or their first month attempting to fix a team they've been on for two years — comes from acting before they've understood what's actually happening. They walk in with a strong opinion about what good looks like, they impose it, and they discover that the team's apparent dysfunction was load-bearing on something they couldn't see.

The cure is observation. Not as a personality trait, not as patience-for-its-own-sake, but as a discipline you do for a defined period before you intervene. A week is usually enough. Sometimes two. The cost of that week is small; the cost of acting wrong is six weeks of cleanup and a team that's stopped trusting you.

This chapter is about how to see.

The principle: light touch

Before the techniques, the principle.

The fixes in this book are the lightest moves that produce the largest changes. That phrase is doing real work. *Lightest* means the move costs the team the least amount of disruption, learning, and political capital. *Largest changes* means the move unblocks more than itself.

Light touch isn't passivity. It's the opposite. A heavy touch — a transformation programme, a SAFe rollout, a team restructure — looks decisive but is usually a failure to understand which lever actually moves the work. You pull thirty levers because you don't know which one matters. The skilled move is to find the one lever that does and pull only that.

Finding it requires observation. The effort in this book is in finding the lever, not in pulling it. That's why Part 1 is about diagnosis before Part 3 is about fixes. If you skip to Part 3 without doing the work in Part 1, you'll pick the wrong fix, apply it confidently, and break things you didn't know were holding the team together.

Three operating mantras come from this principle.

Observe first. You don't yet know the team well enough to know what the load-bearing parts are. The board is messy because the PO is on leave for a month. The standup runs long because the senior developer is mentoring a junior in front of everyone deliberately. The retro is recycling complaints because last quarter the team did something about them and got slapped down. Watch before you intervene.

Ask, don't tell. When you spot something that looks wrong, your first move is a question, not a correction. "Why does this column have eight cards in it?" not "you've got too much WIP." The deeper version of this isn't tactical, it's structural — most teams contain a lot of capable people who have been told what to do for so long that they've stopped trusting their own judgment. Every time you tell, you reinforce that. Every time you ask, you give them a chance to see the problem themselves and own the answer. We'll come back to this in the trust chapter.

Don't interfere with people's work. The team has been doing the job before you arrived (or before you decided to start changing things). Some of them are good at it. Your job is to help work move, not to nitpick how individuals do theirs. If a developer has a process you find inefficient, leave it alone for now. There are bigger fish.

These three principles aren't about being passive. They're about not making the kind of mistakes that take six weeks to recover from. "I want to understand how things work here before I propose changes" is a fully legitimate thing to say out loud, and it buys you the time to actually be useful.

So what are you observing?

A note for readers who aren't new

Most books like this assume you've just walked in. That's a useful frame for the consultant taking on a new engagement, or the manager joining a new company, but it's an unhelpful frame for everyone else.

If you've been on this team for two years, the activity in this chapter is exactly the same. The difference is that you have an advantage and a disadvantage. The advantage is that you already know the people, the politics, and the history. You can skip the bit where you learn names and figure out who the change-makers are. The disadvantage is that you're embedded — your assumptions are part of the system you're trying to see, and you've stopped noticing things that a stranger would clock in five minutes.

The fix for the disadvantage is to deliberately re-elicit. Look at the board as if you'd just arrived. Watch a standup as a stranger would. Ask the questions in the one-on-one section even of people you've worked with for two years. Run the retro as if the team has never done one. The activity is the same; the discipline is forcing yourself to see the system without your usual filters.

The signal that you need to do this isn't that you've started a new job. It's that something has changed and the team's current shape doesn't match the work it's being asked to do. New leadership. A failed quarter. An AI tooling rollout that didn't land. A senior person leaving. Or just the slow accumulation of process that's made the team's velocity drop without any obvious cause. When that happens, run this chapter. Whether you've been there a week or four years.

Talk to everyone

The boards and standups will tell you what's broken. The people will tell you why, and which of them want it fixed.

Have a one-on-one with every member of the team. Not a formal interview, not a "skip-level," just thirty minutes of conversation with no agenda you announce. The agenda you actually have is two questions and a read on the person.

The questions are these:

"What's the most annoying part of getting your work done here?"

"If you could change one thing about how the team works, what would it be?"

Listen to the answers. Don't fix anything yet. Notice when three people independently name the same thing — that's your most leveraged target, even if it's not what you would have picked. The people who do the work always know where the bottleneck is. They've usually given up on it being fixable.

The read you're getting on the person is harder to articulate but more important. You're trying to figure out who on the team is a change-maker and who has accepted the status quo. Both are legitimate — change-makers are exhausting in steady-state environments, and status-quo people keep things running while you're off chasing the next problem — but you need to know who's who. The change-makers are who you'll work through to actually shift things. The status-quo folks are who you don't blindside.

You can usually tell within fifteen minutes. The change-maker leans forward when you ask the second question and lists three things. The status-quo person says "honestly, it's not bad, we just need more people" or "the process works fine, it's just that leadership keeps changing direction." Neither answer is wrong. They're telling you who they are.

You're also reading something else — whether the team can name dysfunction or has stopped seeing it. "We tried that and it didn't work" is a different signal from "we've never been allowed to do that," which is different from "honestly, things are fine." The first means the team has tried and been defeated; the second means the team has been blocked structurally; the third means the team has stopped noticing. Each implies a different mode for what comes next.

Then go up. Talk to whoever's accountable for the team's outcomes — the engineering manager, the CTO, the head of product. Ask them one question:

"What's the single biggest problem you need this team to solve?"

That answer is your political cover. It tells you what the people above the team are paying attention to, which means it tells you what improvements will get noticed and supported, and which improvements will just be noise. If the CTO says "we need to ship the migration this quarter," then your interventions need to visibly serve that. If the head of product says "the team can't seem to make decisions," then you've been told the brief explicitly — and you've also been told that the person above you sees the same problem you do, which is enormously useful. If the answer is vague or contradicts what the team is telling you, that's also data: you've found a misalignment between what the team thinks they're doing and what they're being paid to do, and that's often the deepest problem in the room.

Two things to be careful of. First, don't tell the team what the brief from above was. That's not betrayal — it's just that hearing "the CTO told me X" makes the team feel surveilled, and you're trying to build the opposite of that. The brief is for you. Second, don't tell the higher-ups what the team told you in the one-on-ones. Same reason inverted. The trust you're building goes both directions and depends on both directions staying confidential.

What you do is hold both pictures in your head and find the intervention that serves both. The team wants the recurring meeting killed. The CTO wants the migration shipped. If you can credibly argue that killing the meeting frees four hours a week of senior engineering time that goes into the migration, you have an action that both sides will support, and you didn't have to tell either of them what the other one said.

That's the job. Not observing — anyone can observe. Translating between two groups of people who have the same problem and are describing it in different languages.

The standup

Most of what you need to know about a team is visible in their standup.

Show up to the first one and don't run it. Let whoever has been running it run it. Watch where people look when they speak. If they're all looking at one person — usually the manager or a tech lead — the standup is a status report, not a coordination meeting. The team is reporting up, not synchronising sideways. That's a decision-throughput problem with a name, and you'll see it in plenty of teams.

Watch what gets discussed and what doesn't. If three developers report progress on three different cards and nobody asks each other a clarifying question, the team isn't actually using the standup to align — they're using it to inform an authority figure that work is happening. If someone says "blocked on X" and nothing happens about it, the standup isn't unblocking anyone, it's documenting blockages.

Time it. If the standup runs over twenty minutes, something else is going on. Either decisions are being made in the meeting that should have been made elsewhere, which means there's no other forum for them and decision throughput is concentrated in this 20-minute window. Or status reporting is happening at length, which means someone needs the report and isn't getting it from any other source. Both are bottleneck signals.

The really interesting question is what happens *after* the standup. Do people split off into coordination conversations? Do blockers get resolved in the next hour? Or does everyone go back to their desks and the blocker that was raised at 9:15 is still there at 4:30? The answer tells you whether the standup is doing any work at all.

The board

The board is the team's nervous system. If you can read it, you can read most of the team's pathology without asking anyone anything.

The board's first job is to be a tool the team uses to manage its own work. When it's working, the team is moving cards, asking each other questions about cards, redrawing columns when the workflow changes. When it's not working, the team is treating the board as something they have to update for the manager — a monitoring instrument rather than a tool. You can usually tell within a minute of looking at it. A team's tool is messy, alive, slightly inconsistent, and accurate. A monitoring instrument is tidy, well-formatted, and lying.

The board should represent the actual workflow, not an idealised one. If the team hands off to QA, there's a column for QA. If a PO has to sign off before something ships, there's a column for that. Any step that exists in real life and not on the board is a step where work disappears — it's not visible, you can't measure it, and you can't see when it's stuck. A board that doesn't match the workflow forces the team to lie about where things are.

What you're looking for, in rough priority order:

How many cards are "in progress." If a five-person team has fifteen cards in progress, no card is moving, because nobody is finishing anything. That's not a discipline failure. It's usually a sign that work keeps getting blocked partway through and people are starting new things rather than waiting. Why does work keep blocking partway through? Usually decisions.

How long things have been in their current column. Most boards have something that's been "in review" for three weeks. Click on it. Read the comments. The PR is open, the reviewer was on holiday, nobody picked it up, and now the original author has switched contexts twice and is dreading going back. That's decision debt, in card form. There will be five of these. Take note of who they're stuck on — it usually rhymes.

What's in the leftmost columns. If the backlog and "ready for development" columns are full of items with no acceptance criteria, vague titles, and no recent activity, the team isn't being fed. Engineers can't pick up work that hasn't been decided on. They'll either pick it up anyway and ask clarifying questions later (creating mid-flight rework) or skip it for something more concrete, leaving the high-priority-but-undefined items to age.

Whether the board has a "blocked" column. Most boards do. They probably shouldn't. The existence of the column tells you the team has accepted that some portion of the work will get pulled into progress and stall, and they've built infrastructure to absorb it. That infrastructure makes the underlying problem worse — the team learns that it's fine to pick up work with obvious decision debt baked in, because if it stalls mid-flight, there's a column for that.

The right move is the opposite. If a card doesn't have a clear path to done — missing acceptance criteria, an unmade decision upstream, an unanswered question — it doesn't go into progress. It goes back to the left to be refined first. The same applies if a card gets pulled and then stalls. What teams call "blocked" is usually one of two things: a decision-debt card that should have been refined first, or a card waiting on something the team can actually get if they push for it — system access, a credential, a clarification. The first is a refinement failure. The second isn't blocked, it's delayed. Either way the answer is the same: push it back to the left, not park it on the right.

At a car factory you don't knowingly stamp a bonnet out of rusted metal and hope the rust comes off before paint. Software teams do the equivalent every day and then act surprised when the card sits in "blocked" for two weeks.

Don't take a chance and pull through. This isn't a Hollywood movie where the underdog baseball team makes it through on luck. Luck isn't a workflow. Always have a path to victory before you pick the work up. The blocked column is luck infrastructure.

Whether anyone owns the board. If the standup runs without anyone moving cards, anyone questioning who's working on what, anyone caring about the order from left to right — the board isn't a tool, it's a wall decoration. The team has decoupled their actual work from their visible work, which means you can't use the board to understand them. You'll have to use conversations instead, which is slower.

The backlog

The backlog tells you about decision throughput at the *upstream* end — how good the team is at being given clear, decided, ready-to-build work.

Open it. Sort by date created. Look at the bottom of the list. How old is the oldest item? Six months? Two years? Older?

Now look at who created it. Are they people who still work there? If a meaningful chunk of your backlog is tickets from people who left, that's a fossil layer. The team is sitting on top of decisions that nobody alive made or remembers. They're not going to refine those tickets, and the tickets are going to keep showing up in refinement sessions and getting deferred until eventually someone bulk-archives them in a fit of cleanup energy.

Read ten random tickets from the middle of the backlog. Can you tell what each one is asking for? If you can't, the team can't either. Vague tickets are decision debt — someone made a half-decision (we should do X) and then deferred the rest of the decision (here's exactly what X means and here's what done looks like). That deferred decision will get made by whoever picks up the ticket, under pressure, in the worst conditions.

Count the unrefined tickets. If there are four hundred, it's a graveyard. The team is using the backlog as a place to put ideas they don't want to throw away, not as a queue of work that's actually going to happen. There's no cost difference to anyone of marking a ticket "won't do," but there's a perceived political cost — it might offend whoever raised it, or signal that the team isn't ambitious enough. So the tickets accumulate. The team has lost the ability to make the small decision of "no, we won't do this" thousands of times over.

Cards are inventory. Refined cards are inventory that's been through a value-adding process — someone clarified scope, someone wrote acceptance criteria, someone agreed what done looks like. That refinement is paid for in time, and like any inventory, it depreciates. Time erodes value. Six months on, the ticket the team carefully refined no longer matches the system it's meant to apply to, and the investment is gone.

The 400-ticket backlog isn't just messy. It's a depreciation event in slow motion. The team's most valuable refinement work is sitting in the lower half of the list, ageing into uselessness, while they refine new tickets to put on top. The same logic applies to documentation: most of it is a depreciating asset, accurate the day it was written and increasingly wrong after. Don't invest heavily in a depreciating asset. Refine just-in-time, document what changes least, and accept that yesterday's careful work is today's noise.

Who's deciding what

This is the most important observation and the hardest, because it's not in any ticketing system. You have to put it together from listening.

Every time something gets stuck, ask yourself: who has to decide this for it to move? Then watch how long the decision takes.

You'll see patterns fast. There's usually one person whose name comes up in three different blocking conversations. The PO who needs to clarify acceptance criteria. The architect whose review is required before any backend change. The CTO whose sign-off is required for anything customer-facing. The compliance officer who lives in another department and answers email twice a week.

These people aren't villains. They're often very competent and very overloaded. The question isn't whether they're bad at their job; it's whether the system has accidentally arranged for too many decisions to flow through them. Once you see it, you'll see it everywhere — the same person's name on five different stuck cards.

This is your bottleneck, in the Goldratt sense. Not the slow developer. Not the immature CI pipeline. Not the buggy test environment. Those are noise. The actual constraint is the person, or sometimes the meeting, or the approval workflow, or the document that requires three signatures, that everything is queued behind.

You're not going to fix this immediately. You're going to see it.

The retro

The fourth elicitation technique, and the one that does work the others can't: surfacing what people only say when they hear someone else say it first.

Toward the end of the observation period, run the team's retro. If the team already has a retro on the calendar, you're using that one. If they don't, you're putting one on. Either way, this is now the team's regular retro — not a one-off workshop. The format is the same one you'll run every cadence after this. The only thing that makes the first one different is its scope: it covers everything since you arrived, which is usually a week or two of accumulated material. Later retros only cover the period since the last retro, which is usually a sprint or a fortnight.

Because the first one is covering more ground, it runs longer — block out ninety minutes. Subsequent retros are shorter; an hour is usually plenty. Same format, smaller window. You can run it on a wall, a whiteboard, or a Miro board if you're remote.

Phase one is brain-dump. Give everyone fifteen minutes to write pain points on stickies. One pain per sticky. No filtering, no editing, no judgement about whether it's the team's fault or the org's fault or anyone's fault. Just things that make the work harder than it should be.

Phase two is grouping. Cluster the stickies on the wall. Most of them will fall into four or five themes naturally. Don't force it; if a sticky doesn't fit, leave it on its own.

Phase three is the matrix. Draw two axes — *impact* (low to high) on one, *effort* (low to high) on the other. Get the team to place each pain point or theme cluster onto the matrix. The discussion that happens during placement is more valuable than the matrix itself. People argue about whether something is high-impact or not, and in the arguing, things get said that wouldn't have been said in a one-on-one because the speaker didn't think the rest of the team would agree. They do agree. Now everyone knows.

The high-impact / low-effort quadrant is where you focus. That's the fix list — the things the team itself has identified as the leverage points.

Two things to do during the placement that aren't on the standard playbook:

Highlight things they're not seeing. You've been observing for a week. There will be at least one dysfunction you've identified that nobody on the team raises in the brain-dump phase. You don't impose it on the matrix yourself. You raise it in discussion. "I've noticed X — what's the team's read on whether that belongs up there?" If they agree, it goes on. If they don't, you have two options: drop it (they're closer to the work than you are, they may be right) or add it as a placeholder with a note that you'll come back to it. The second option is honest about your disagreement without overriding their priority list.

Separate what they fix from what you fix. Some items on the matrix are theirs to fix — the recurring meeting that doesn't work, the way they run refinement, the team's working agreements. Some items are yours, because they require authority the team doesn't have — pushing back on a deadline the CTO has set, getting headcount approved, getting the team access to a paid tool the budget doesn't currently cover. Mark them differently. The team owns the team list. You own the upstream list. This split matters because the team needs to see that you're going to do real work on items they can't reach, and they need to feel ownership over the items they can.

The output is a prioritised list the team produced, with you as the facilitator. They own it. They'll act on it because they own it. And you have a parallel list of things you'll work on that they can't, which you'll report progress on so they know you're holding up your end.

If the brain-dump produces nothing, or the matrix discussion stays superficial, or nobody will say anything controversial — that's not the retro failing. It's the retro doing its job. It's showing you something about the team's current relationship with the format, usually that they've stopped investing because retros haven't produced change in a long time. That's diagnostic data, and the next chapter is partly about what to do with it.

The five things you'll see

After the observation period, you'll have spotted some version of the following. The names matter less than the patterns; you'll come to recognise them on sight.

The status standup. The team gathers daily to report progress to a manager or stakeholder rather than coordinate with each other. Decisions made in the meeting: zero. Information distributed: redundant.

The decision graveyard. The backlog is enormous, mostly old, mostly vague, and refined only when someone needs to find a ticket to drop a "won't do" comment on. Decisions made: minimal. Decisions deferred indefinitely: thousands.

The sign-off chokepoint. All work passes through one or two people for approval. They're competent, conscientious, and overloaded. Work piles up behind them. The rest of the team has accidentally built their workflow around their colleague's calendar.

The escalation reflex. The PO or product manager doesn't make decisions; they relay questions upward and decisions downward. Every clarification takes a day or three. The team has learned not to ask, which means they ship the version they assumed was correct and rework it later.

The recycled retro. The same complaints surface every fortnight. The team raises them, the team agrees something should be done, nothing happens, the team raises them again. Over time the team stops believing the retro can produce change. They keep attending because it's mandatory.

You'll see at least three of these in any team. You'll often see all five. They aren't separate problems — they're the same problem expressed five ways. The decision throughput is too low for the work the team is being asked to do.

The lens: waste

Every pattern above is a kind of waste. The status standup wastes the team's time on coordination that isn't happening. The decision graveyard wastes refinement effort on tickets that will never ship. The sign-off chokepoint wastes everyone behind it. The escalation reflex wastes time on clarifications that should have been decided already. The recycled retro wastes the most valuable ceremony the team has.

That's the lens this book is built on. The job isn't to add new processes, ceremonies, or roles — the job is to find the waste in the team's system and remove it. Most software delivery problems look complicated until you ask *what's being wasted here?* and then they look like waste hiding behind a process nobody can quite remember why the team agreed to.

Lean has a vocabulary for this — the seven wastes, *muda, mura, muri.* You can read about it elsewhere. This book uses plain English. The question is always the same. Where is work waiting that doesn't need to wait? Where is effort going into things that won't ship? Where is capability being held back by something the team could remove if it noticed it? The rescue chapters in Part 3 are, fundamentally, waste-elimination moves. The trust chapter coming next is about the deepest waste — the capability that already exists in the team but is being suppressed by a system that has stopped trusting it.

What to do with what you've seen

You now have two pictures.

Yours: the four observation surfaces (standup, board, backlog, who's deciding) plus the patterns you've heard in the one-on-ones. This is the diagnosis.

Theirs: the retro produced a prioritised list of pain points the team itself identified. This is the agenda.

The next chapter is about reconciling these two pictures and picking what to act on. Sometimes they overlap perfectly and the answer is obvious. Sometimes they don't — you've seen something the team didn't surface, or the team has prioritised something you think isn't the real lever, or the retro itself was low-energy and the prioritised list is thin. The mode you operate in for the weeks that follow depends on which of those situations you're in.

What you don't do, ever, is announce your diagnosis as a list of dysfunctions you've identified. "I've found five things wrong with how this team works and here's my plan" is the wrong move whether you've been there a week or two years. The team will hear "the new guy thinks we're broken" or "this person who I thought was on my side has been judging us" and the rest of your tenure will be uphill. The diagnosis is for you. The actions are visible; the analysis behind them is not.

You also don't try to do all five. The temptation is real — you can see all the problems, you have the levers in this book, why not pull them all? Because pulling five levers at once means none of them get the attention they need, the team experiences it as chaos rather than improvement, and you lose the ability to tell which intervention actually worked. Pick one. Make it work. Move to the next.

Light touch. The smallest move that produces the largest change. That's what the next chapter is about.

Chapter 2: Picking What to Act On

MOST teams fail here not because they pick the wrong thing to fix, but because they try to fix everything at once.

You walked out of the retro on Friday with two artifacts. The team's prioritised list of things they want to fix, ordered by impact and effort. And your private notebook from the week of observation, which has things in it the team didn't surface.

Now what.

The temptation is to merge the two lists into one master list and start working through it. Don't. The two lists are different *kinds* of work and they get handled differently. The team's list is theirs to lead on. Your list — the things they couldn't see, or things only you have the authority to address — is yours. They run in parallel. The first chapter set this up. This one shows you how to actually run them.

Open by default

Process is open. That's the operating rule, and almost everything in this chapter follows from it.

If the team produced a fix list in the retro, the work to act on that list happens in the open. The team can see what's being worked on, who's leading each item, and what progress looks like. They can disagree, suggest changes, raise problems. They can see when something's stuck. The whole point of the retro was to surface the team's own diagnosis; running the action in the open is just the consistent application of that.

There are exceptions, and they're worth naming up front so you don't accidentally drift into being secretive.

Closed-door managerial work stays closed. Team redesigns. Performance conversations. Hiring or firing decisions. Structural changes to roles or reporting lines. These are quiet because they're not the team's business anyway — they affect the team but the team isn't a participant in the decision, and pretending otherwise would be theatre. If you're a delivery manager without authority over these, you're not doing them; if you are doing them, do them through the proper channels and don't dress them up as collaborative.

Items the team can't action. If the retro surfaced something that requires authority the team doesn't have — pushing back on a deadline the CTO has set, getting headcount approved, getting the team access to a paid tool the budget doesn't currently cover — that goes on your list, not theirs. You work it. You report progress back to the team because they raised it. But you don't pretend they're leading something they can't.

Briefs from above that aren't yours to share. Sometimes leadership tells you something in confidence — usually about strategy, sometimes about people. The action you take on it might still be open work even when the original conversation was private. *I'm working on getting more clarity on the Q3 priorities* is a fine open statement even if the conversation that produced it was private. The disclosure stays private; the action can still be visible.

The default is open. Quiet is for closed-door managerial work. If you find yourself wanting to be neither open nor quiet — hinting at things you're not saying, dropping cryptic references in standup, signalling that you know something the team doesn't — stop. That's worse than either. It creates the surveillance feeling we talked about in Chapter 1 and undermines the trust the open work is building. Pick a lane.

The team's list: who leads, and what leading means

For each item on the team's list, you ask for a volunteer to lead.

Not to *do*. To lead. Those are different jobs and the distinction is the whole point. The leader's job is to make sure the item gets actioned. They don't have to write the code, run the new ceremony, or be the one who closes the PRs. They have to ensure the work is happening, unblock it when it stalls, and keep the rest of the team informed about progress.

The volunteer model matters more than it looks. When the team self-selects leaders, three things happen. The work gets owned by someone who actually wants to own it, which is a much stronger predictor of completion than someone being assigned to it. The leader develops or exercises a skill they wouldn't have otherwise. And the team learns that the items on the matrix are theirs — that you're not running a programme of changes that they're being subjected to, you're supporting changes they're driving.

If nobody volunteers for an item, that's information. It might mean the item isn't actually as high-priority as the matrix suggested. It might mean nobody believes the item can be fixed. It might mean the people who'd naturally lead it are already too stretched. Have a conversation about why before defaulting to assigning someone. If you assign a leader who didn't volunteer, you've reverted to the management-by-decree pattern the retro was supposed to undo.

If nobody volunteers and the conversation about why doesn't surface a leader either, the move isn't to wait. Pick something — anything from the matrix — and start it. Throw your observation at the wall. *I'm noticing this thing. Anyone want to take it on?* Most of the time someone pipes up, even if they wouldn't have raised their hand cold. Sometimes nobody does, and you randomly pick someone to lead. There's a name for this — voluntold. Make the randomness visible. I've used a spinning wheel with each team member's name on it, projected on the screen. The wheel spins in front of everyone, lands on a name, and that person leads. It sounds silly, but it does two useful jobs: it makes the selection feel fair rather than arbitrary, and it makes *not volunteering* feel like a collective choice the team is making rather than something you'll quietly let pass. That's not ideal, but it's better than waiting for self-selection that isn't going to happen yet. The first item is the one that builds belief that the matrix produces change. After that, volunteers get easier.

Once a leader has volunteered, they decide how progress gets communicated. Some leaders set up a fortnightly fifteen-minute forum on that specific item. Some broadcast updates in standup or in a Slack channel. Some hold off until they have something concrete to report and then make a more substantial update at retro. The format isn't your call. The expectation that *something* gets communicated is — but the leader picks the mechanism that fits the work.

Your job in this whole arrangement is small. You support when asked. You unblock when the leader can't. You hold the larger picture of which items are progressing and which are stuck. You don't run the work. The whole point is that the team is now running their own improvement programme, and you're the one who set it up and stays around to help.

If a leader stalls, the move isn't to take over. The move is to ask. *What's getting in the way? What would help?* Sometimes the answer is "I need more time." Sometimes it's "I don't actually have the authority to do the thing I said I'd do" — which is useful, because it tells you the item belonged on your list, not theirs. Sometimes it's "I've thought about it more and I don't think this is the right fix" — which is also useful, and the team's matrix is a living document, not a contract.

When the team can't yet self-organise: the benevolent dictator mode

The volunteer-leader model assumes the team is willing and able to take ownership of items if the structure lets them. Most teams meet this bar. Some teams don't, yet, and the reason usually isn't capability — it's that they've stopped believing improvement is possible.

If nobody volunteers, the conversation about why doesn't surface a leader, and even the random-pick fallback produces someone who can't get the work moving, you've hit a team that has fully checked out of its own improvement. The volunteer model can't bootstrap from zero. Something has to break the pattern first.

The temporary mode is what the open source world calls the benevolent dictator. You drive the next improvement yourself. You decide what the change is. You make it happen. You report on what changed. The team watches. They don't own this one. You do.

This sounds like exactly the management-by-decree pattern the chapter is built against, and it would be — except for two qualifiers that change everything. First, it's temporary. The first one or two improvements you drive yourself; everything after is back on the volunteer model. Second, the work you pick has to demonstrably make the team's life better in a way they can feel within a sprint. If they can't feel the improvement, you've just confirmed their model that nothing changes. If they can, you've supplied the data that updates that model, and the next item you put on the matrix gets a real volunteer.

The benevolent dictator mode is what you use when a team's learned helplessness is stronger than their willingness to engage with the matrix. It's a way of paying for the next round of trust with your own labour. Use it, get out of it, and don't return to it once the volunteer model starts producing. A manager who stays in benevolent-dictator mode after the team has shown it can self-organise has reverted to the pattern the book is trying to undo.

Your list: what's on it, and how you communicate progress

Your list has the items the team can't action.

Some of these are upstream items that came out of the retro — leadership decisions, cross-team coordination, structural problems. Some are things you've identified privately that you're going to act on without raising them on the matrix yet. Some are briefs from leadership that align with what the team needs.

For each item on your list, the question to answer is: *is this open or quiet?*

It's open if the team raised it, asked for it, or would benefit from knowing you're working on it. The architect chokepoint they identified in the retro is open. The misalignment with the other team that's blocking three of their stories is open. The fact that you're trying to get them more headcount is open if it's real and quiet if you don't yet know whether it's real.

It's quiet if it's a managerial decision the team isn't part of. A team redesign is quiet. A performance conversation about a specific team member is quiet. A confidential strategy briefing from leadership is quiet, though the actions that come out of it might be open.

The reason for naming this distinction is so you communicate appropriately on each. For open items, you make progress visible. Standup mention if it's relevant to the day's work. Retro mention as a standing item — *here's where we're up to on the things from the matrix that are on my list.* Slack updates when there's something to update. The team should never have to ask you what's happening on something they raised; they should know.

For quiet items, you don't communicate progress because the work isn't theirs. Once a quiet decision becomes a real action — a structural change, a personnel move, a new reporting line — it gets communicated through the proper channels at the appropriate time. Until then, you don't reference it.

The thing to avoid is the half-measure: hinting at quiet work, dropping cryptic references in standup, signalling that you know something the team doesn't. That's worse than either being open or staying silent. It creates the surveillance feeling we talked about in Chapter 1 and undermines the trust the open work is building.

The three criteria still apply

Whether you're picking from the team's list or your own, the fix you act on first has to clear three bars.

It has to be cheap. Attemptable inside a single working week, without budget, without hiring, without restructuring, without the team having to learn anything new. Cheap fixes are reversible. If they don't work you can stop doing them and try something else. Expensive fixes commit you to outcomes you can't predict.

It has to be high-leverage. The fix has to unblock more than itself. Killing one meeting is worth doing if it frees four hours of senior engineering time. Adding acceptance criteria to one ticket is worth doing if that ticket is currently blocking three others. The test is: how many other things does this unblock?

The team has to either want it or not notice it. For team list items, this is automatic — they put it on the matrix, they want it. For your list items, this is the rule that keeps you honest. If the move is something the team would resist, it has to be either delayed until they're ready or done quietly through proper channels. The fix that survives long-term is the one the team wanted or the one they didn't notice you'd done. Anything else gets reversed.

In open mode, the team has done some of this work for you in the retro. The high-impact / low-effort quadrant is approximately the cheap-and-leveraged set. The volunteer step handles the wanted-or-unnoticed criterion automatically — if someone volunteered to lead, somebody wants this. Your job is to sense-check the team's prioritisation, raise it if you think they've miscalculated, and otherwise support what they've decided.

In quiet mode — for items on your list — you do the three-criteria evaluation yourself. The discipline is the same. The accountability is to yourself.

When the team's priority isn't the leverage point

You'll see it sometimes. The team has put something in their high-impact / low-effort quadrant that you're pretty sure isn't going to move work, and the actual leverage point is somewhere they've underweighted.

Don't override them. The cost of overriding is higher than the cost of letting them work their priority and finding out.

Three reasons. First, you might be wrong. The team is closer to the work than you are, and the thing they put at the top might be high-impact in a way you can't see yet. Wait two or three weeks and the answer will be clear. Second, even if you're right, the team learning by doing the work is more valuable than the work itself. They run their priority, it doesn't quite produce the unblock they hoped, they ask why, you have a conversation about leverage. Now they understand leverage. Next time they prioritise more accurately. The teaching moment is the actual deliverable. Third, overriding the team's priority is the management-by-decree pattern dressed up as expertise. The retro was set up to put the team in charge of their own diagnosis. Reversing that in week two undoes the trust you just built.

What you can do is raise the alternative without insisting on it. *I noticed this other thing in the standup last week — do we want to put it on the matrix to discuss?* If they agree, it goes on. If they don't, you've raised it and you can come back to it later if it becomes more obviously a problem.

The exception is when the team's priority would actively make things worse. If they've prioritised "switch to a new ticketing system" and you can see that's going to consume three months of attention that the team can't afford, you push back. But that's a different conversation — you're not overriding their judgment about what matters, you're flagging a cost they may have underestimated. *I want to make sure we're clear on what this would cost in time over the next quarter — is that what we want to spend it on?*

Worked examples

Three teams I've seen, and the fix that worked. The names are made up; the patterns are not. I'm tagging each with the mode and list it belonged on.

Team A. Six developers, one PO, internal tooling for a retail company. Standup ran forty minutes. Eighteen cards in progress. The PO seemed competent but tickets sat in "ready for development" for a week before anyone picked them up because the acceptance criteria were always one bullet point that didn't quite say what was wanted.

The team's matrix surfaced "tickets aren't ready when we pick them up" in the high-impact / low-effort quadrant. A senior developer volunteered to lead. The fix she ran was a fifteen-minute pre-refinement session three days a week, where the PO sat with her and walked through the next three tickets, with her asking "what does done look like?" until they had a real answer. Tickets got better. WIP started dropping within ten days. She updated progress at retro every fortnight.

The fix wasn't elegant. Adding a recurring meeting to fix a problem caused by missing detail in tickets is, on its face, the sort of thing this book argues against. But it was the right *first* fix, because what it actually did was teach the PO how to look at tickets ahead of time.

Two sprints in, the bottleneck moved. The sessions were working — tickets came into development with real acceptance criteria — but the PO was now spending most of her week running them, and the rest of the backlog wasn't getting attention. That's not failure. That's the system telling you what to fix next. The team's matrix at the following retro surfaced the next move: the PO would participate in planning differently, bringing what she'd learned about what "done" looks like upstream, so tickets arrived at refinement with the question already half-answered. After about three months the pre-refinement meeting got dropped — she'd absorbed the pattern and was doing it on her own. The version after that was the acceptance criteria being good enough that no conversation was needed at all. The fifteen-minute meeting was scaffolding, not the destination.

Mode: open. List: theirs. Volunteer led the work, then iterated as the PO's capability grew. The bottleneck moved twice in three months — that's the work, not a problem with it. The first fix doesn't have to be elegant; it has to be something the team can absorb and improve on.

Team B. Twelve people across two squads, customer-facing features. The architect on the platform side reviewed every PR that touched the backend. He was thorough, careful, and seven days behind on average.

The team's matrix surfaced "review queue is killing us." The team's instinct was to ask the architect to be faster, which wouldn't have worked. The actual leverage was upstream — the architect was a chokepoint by design after a bad incident two years ago, and only leadership could change that arrangement. I put it on my list, talked to leadership, and we agreed to give two senior developers explicit pre-review responsibility with a checklist before the architect saw it. The architect kept his veto. His turnaround dropped from seven days to one. WIP in review halved within a fortnight.

Mode: open. List: mine, because the team didn't have authority to change a review structure leadership had locked in. I reported progress at retro each fortnight: "I'm working with [VP of Engineering] on the pre-review structure, here's where we're up to."

Team C. Five developers, one product manager, B2B platform. The retro had been running the same five complaints for eight months. The team was demoralised. The PM was new and the previous one had left under bad circumstances.

The retro was low-energy. The team brain-dumped fine but the placement phase was thin — most things ended up in the high-effort, low-impact quadrant ("things won't change anyway"). Few volunteers stepped forward.

That's data, not failure. The retro worked exactly as it was supposed to: it showed me that retros generally weren't producing change for this team. They'd stopped investing in the format because nothing came out of it. The fix isn't to give up on the retro — it's to make it earn the team's investment back.

I picked something that had come out of the matrix anyway — close PRs within 48 hours — and ran it. The volunteer didn't quite materialise on its own, so I raised the observation in standup: *I'm noticing nobody's picked this up. What's going on?* One of the developers said the PR backlog was killing him personally and offered to lead it. He led, it got done in a sprint. At the next retro, I named what had happened — the thing we said we'd do, we did, and here's what changed. Someone else volunteered for the next thing. By the third retro, the team had started raising new complaints because the old ones were getting resolved, and the next retro had a much higher-energy placement phase.

Mode: open. List: started as mine to drive, shifted to theirs as the volunteer model took hold. The retro didn't fail — it told me which fix to start with.

How to know if it worked

The test isn't whether the team likes you better, or whether the standup feels different, or whether someone said something nice in the retro.

The test is whether work moved that wouldn't have moved otherwise.

Define this before you start. For each item being worked, identify one or two specific cards or items that, if the fix works, will visibly move within the next two weeks. The PR that's been in review for nine days. The story that's been "ready for development" for three weeks because the AC isn't clear. The bug that's been deprioritised in three consecutive sprints. If those things move, the fix worked. If they don't, the fix didn't work, regardless of how it felt.

Keep a list. It can be a Slack message to yourself, a sticky note, anything. Just write down which cards you expect to move and when. Two weeks later, check.

This is a discipline that almost nobody in this profession maintains, and it's why most interventions are unfalsifiable. Workshops get run, teams feel good, the workshop is declared a success, and a month later nothing has actually changed. You're doing the opposite. The intervention either moved the named cards or it didn't. There's no in-between and there's no negotiating with the data.

If the fix didn't work — and roughly a third of the time it won't, even when you've picked carefully — the move is to stop doing it, not to double down. Tell the team (or the leader of that item) what you expected and what didn't happen. Have an honest conversation about why. Sometimes the answer is "we didn't actually do the thing we said we'd do," which is itself useful. Sometimes it's "we did it but the constraint was somewhere else." Sometimes it's "the system pushed back in a way we didn't expect." All three responses point at different next moves.

The reason a third of fixes fail isn't that you picked wrong; it's that the team is a system, and systems push back on changes in ways you can't always predict. The fifteen-minute pre-refinement session helps Team A and would be sabotaged by a different PO who hates having her writing critiqued. Same fix, different outcomes. Stop, learn, pick again.

When to pick the next thing

You don't pick the next thing until the current one has either worked or definitively failed.

This is the rule everyone breaks. They start one fix, see it taking effect, get excited, start a second fix in week three. The second fix lands in a system that's already changing, you can't tell which intervention is responsible for what, and if either one fails subtly you won't know. The team also experiences it as constant change, which is exhausting.

Wait. Let the first fix bed in for at least three weeks. Watch the named cards. Notice whether the dysfunction has softened or just moved. Some fixes look like they worked but actually displaced the constraint somewhere else — the architect is unblocked, but now the senior developer doing pre-review has become the new bottleneck. That's not failure, but it changes what the next fix should be.

"Worked" doesn't mean "done." The fix you've installed is a starting point, not a destination. Once it's bedded in, ask whether it can be simplified, retired, or replaced with something the team can sustain unaided. Team A's pre-refinement meeting was scaffolding — once the PO had absorbed the pattern, the meeting got dropped. She didn't need the meeting; she needed to learn the habit, and the meeting was how she learned. You meet the team where they are, install the lightest thing that works, and iterate from there as their capability grows. Continuous improvement isn't a slogan — it's the discipline of returning to the fix and asking what the lighter version is. The first fix doesn't have to be perfect. It has to be an incremental improvement the team can build on.

For team-list items, the leader of the current item decides when it's complete. They report it as done, the team confirms, the next item gets a volunteer leader. For your list items, you decide. Same discipline either way: don't move on until you can name what changed.

By the time the team has worked through three or four items, you'll have a pattern. The team will be visibly faster. Recurring complaints will be resolved or replaced with new ones. The board will look different. People will start telling you things they noticed that they think you should look at. That's the inflection point — the team has started doing the diagnosis with you, instead of waiting to see what you'll do next.

That's where you want to get to. Not in week two. Probably not in week six either. But it gets there if you pick well, one item at a time, with leaders who own the work.

The next chapter is about the principle behind all of this. Why the open mode works. Why the volunteer model produces better outcomes than assignment. Why the manager who gets out of the way produces faster delivery than the manager who runs every decision. The trust problem.

Chapter 3: Trust as the Operating Principle

EVERY team you'll work with has the same trust failure, expressed in cards.

A developer who could decide something without escalating, but doesn't. A PO who could pick the next priority, but waits for confirmation. An architect who could approve a PR in five minutes, but takes a week. They aren't slow people. They're cautious people, and the caution is rational. Somewhere upstream, a decision someone made cost them — got reversed, got criticised, got blamed when something went wrong — and the rational response is to stop deciding without cover.

Multiply that across a team, then across an organisation, then across a few years, and you have a system in which the smartest people in the building have collectively learned that the safest move is to defer. The decisions still have to happen, but they happen further up the chain, where they take longer, lose context, and arrive back at the team along with the sense that the team didn't really do its job.

That's the trust problem the introduction promised to come back to. This is the chapter that comes back to it.

The first two chapters told you how to see the system and pick what to act on. They didn't tell you why the moves work. The volunteer-leader model, the open-by-default rule, the team owning its own diagnosis, the manager getting out of the way — these aren't arbitrary preferences. They're specific, operational consequences of a single thesis: the constraint on software delivery is decision throughput, decision throughput is gated by trust, and trust can be rebuilt through behaviour faster than through any culture programme you've ever seen.

This chapter explains why. It also gives you the moves to do it on Monday.

Trust is not a feeling

The first thing to do is take the word back from the coaching industry.

Trust isn't psychological safety. It isn't vulnerability. It isn't "feeling heard" or "being seen." Those things matter — and good coaches help with them — but they're consequences, not causes, and treating them as causes is how delivery work gets endless intangible advice that doesn't act on anything.

Trust, in the operational sense this book uses, is **predictable autonomy**.

A team trusts you when they can predict three things: what you'll do, when you'll do it, and that you'll actually do what you said. Not what you intended. Not what you hoped. What happened. Predictability is the load-bearing element — the team doesn't need you to be reliably nice or reliably patient, they need you to be reliable. A manager who is unpleasant but predictable is more trusted than a manager who is pleasant but unpredictable, because the team can plan around the first one.

You trust the team when you stop checking on things you've delegated.

That's the test. Not how you feel about the people. Not whether you'd hire them again. Whether you actually let them run the thing without looking over their shoulder, intervening at the last minute, asking for status updates that the open progress channels would have given you anyway. If you've delegated something and you're still pinging the leader for updates, you haven't actually delegated it.

Both directions of trust are observable. Both are falsifiable. Both can be rebuilt through specific moves rather than through culture work.

That's why this chapter exists. Trust as a feeling is a slow target. Trust as predictable autonomy is operationally addressable on Monday.

Decision debt is trust debt

In the introduction we called it decision debt — the accumulation of approval gates, sign-offs, and escalations that organisations build one good reason at a time. Here's what's actually frozen inside each one of them: a moment when somebody's autonomy got revoked.

The architect didn't lose his decision-making authority because somebody decided architects shouldn't decide. He lost it because two years ago a decision he made — fine at the time, given what he knew — caused an incident, and the organisational response was to add review. The PO doesn't escalate because she's incapable. She escalates because the time she made a call without checking, leadership reversed it publicly and made her look bad in front of the team. The senior developer doesn't push back on the deadline because the last person who did got branded as "not a team player."

Each of those is rational caution learned from a specific event, written into the system as a process, and never removed when the conditions that justified it changed. That's what process is, mostly: frozen distrust, preserved in policy, long after the moment that froze it has passed.

You can't fix this by telling the team to be more confident. The caution is correct given what they've experienced. The fix is to actually behave differently, consistently, for long enough that the data updates — to give the architect cover when he makes a call, to back the PO when she's right and have the conversation in private when she's wrong, to push back yourself on the deadline so the senior developer doesn't have to.

This is also why "build a culture of psychological safety" workshops don't work. The psychological state isn't the input. The behaviour is the input. The state follows. A team that has been burned will tell you they want safety, will write it on workshop stickies, and will still escalate every decision the next morning, because they've been burned and they don't yet have the data that says you're different. They'll get that data only by watching what you do.

The lever is behaviour. Repeated. Consistent. In public.

The two directions

Trust flows in two directions. Up: the team trusts you. Down: you trust the team. Most management writing focuses on the second. In practice, the first one matters more, because it's the precondition for everything else.

The team observes you constantly. They notice what you do with information they give you in private. They notice whether you defend them in meetings they're not in. They notice whether your stated priorities match what you actually spend time on. They notice when you say you'll follow up on something and don't. They notice all of this without meaning to. A team that has worked together for a year has a very accurate model of every manager they've had, and that model was built by accumulating tiny observations, not by reading the manager's stated values.

The first direction of trust — them trusting you — is built by accumulating those observations in the right direction. Every promise kept moves the needle a tiny amount. Every promise broken moves it a bigger amount. The asymmetry is brutal: trust takes weeks to build and minutes to lose. That's not weakness on the team's part. It's a rational response to a long history in which the trust they extended was repeatedly punished.

Two specific moves build this direction faster than anything else.

The first is private confidentiality. What was said in a one-on-one stays in the one-on-one. What leadership told you in confidence stays in confidence — full stop, including not hinting at it, including not signalling that you know something the team doesn't. We covered this in chapter 2 under the half-measure rule. It applies here too. The team finds out fast whether you can keep a confidence, and once they're sure you can, they tell you the things you actually need to know to be useful.

The second is public defence. When something gets attributed to the team that wasn't their fault — a missed deadline that was actually a scope change from above, a quality issue caused by an upstream decision they raised concerns about, a metric that doesn't measure what people think it measures — your job is to clarify, in the room, in front of the people who matter. Not later. Not in a Slack message after. In the room. The team finds out fast whether you'll do this, and the answer determines whether they'll bring you the next thing that matters before it gets to that point.

The second direction — you trusting them — is operationally simpler. You ask for volunteers and let the volunteers run the work. You delegate and stop checking. When the leader of an item says it's done, it's done. You don't have a separate private definition of done that you apply later.

This is harder than it sounds, because the instinct is the opposite. You see the leader is working differently than you would, and you intervene. You see them missing something you'd have noticed, and you flag it. Both interventions are subtle distrust signals, even if they're well-meant, and the team picks them up immediately. The discipline is to intervene only when the open-progress signals say there's a real problem — the named cards aren't moving, the fortnightly update has gone silent, the leader has admitted they're stuck — and to do nothing the rest of the time.

If you can't do nothing, you don't actually trust them. And if you don't, they know.

How open mode rebuilds trust

The first two chapters told you to operate in open mode. Here's the mechanic.

Open mode makes your behaviour predictable. The team can see what's being worked on, who's leading what, and where each item stands. They can see your private upstream list and how it's progressing, because you report on it visibly. They can see the closed-door work isn't there, and they know where the line sits between the open and the quiet, because you've drawn it explicitly.

Predictability is the prerequisite for trust. When the team can predict what you'll do, when you'll do it, and what you've already done, the data they need to update their model of you is being supplied continuously. Every visible action is a tiny piece of evidence. Over weeks, the model updates. The team starts to operate as if the new model is correct — which manifests as them deciding things without escalating, raising concerns earlier, volunteering for items, telling you problems before they're crises.

Hidden mode does the opposite. When work is being done in private, the team can't update its model, so the model that gets used is the historical one, which was built from previous managers and is usually worse than the reality. They assume the worst because they have no data to do anything else. This is why the manager who runs everything quietly for "good reasons" produces a more anxious team than the manager who runs the same things openly. The information vacuum gets filled with the team's prior bad experiences.

The exception we drew in chapter 2 — closed-door managerial work stays closed — is not a contradiction. It's the boundary that makes the openness credible. If everything is open, the team starts to suspect that the things you can't talk about aren't being handled at all. If most things are open and a small set of clearly-categorised things are closed, the team can tell which is which, and the closed set isn't ambiguous. The architect's pre-review discussion with the VP of Engineering is open. The conversation about whether to manage someone out is closed. The team understands the difference and doesn't have to guess.

This is also why hinting at quiet work — the half-measure — is so corrosive. It collapses the distinction between open and closed and replaces it with "the manager knows things you don't," which is the worst of both worlds. The team has the information vacuum and the awareness that you're filling it without them.

The volunteer model as operational trust

In chapter 2 you learned the procedure: ask for a volunteer, let the volunteer lead, get out of the way. Here's what it's actually doing.

Asking for a volunteer is a public statement that the team contains the right person to lead this work, you don't yet know who, and you trust them collectively to self-select. That's a strong statement, made operationally rather than verbally. The team hears it the same way they'd hear "I trust you" — except they don't have to take your word for it, because the proof is in the procedure itself.

Letting the volunteer lead is the second statement. You're not picking the work pattern, the schedule, the format, or the milestones. The volunteer is. They get to be wrong in the small ways they will inevitably be wrong, learn from it, adjust, and own the result. The model treats them as a competent adult who has taken on a leadership role and gets to exercise it.

Getting out of the way is the third. The visible signal that you mean what the first two said. Not asking for status, not pinging for updates, not nudging in standup, not gently steering in side conversations. Holding the position that the named cards will move or won't, the leader will report at the cadence they've set, and your role is to support when asked, not to manage by proximity.

This is hard. Almost everyone fails it the first few times. The instinct to nudge is strong, especially when you can see something the leader can't, or when you're nervous about delivery. The discipline is to recognise that the nudge undoes the trust statement you made when you asked for the volunteer. If you have a real concern, you have a real conversation, in the open, framed as a question rather than a direction. *Here's what I'm seeing — what's your read?* If you don't have a real concern and you're just anxious, the right move is to do nothing.

A team that watches you do this consistently learns something about you that culture work could never teach. They learn that when you delegate, you actually delegate. The next item gets a faster volunteer.

What breaks trust

The trust you've built breaks faster than it accumulated. Some specific failures are recoverable, and some aren't. Knowing the difference matters.

The recoverable ones are usually a single broken commitment. You said you'd follow up on the architect conversation by Friday and you didn't. You said the upstream item was open and you stopped reporting on it. You said you'd defend the team's position with leadership and you ducked when it came time. These cost real trust, and the cost is bigger than you'll feel from the inside, because the team's prior data set predicts that they'll be punished for raising it.

Recovery is straightforward but specific. You name the failure, in the open, before they raise it. *I said I'd follow up on the architect conversation by Friday and I haven't. Here's why, here's what I'm doing now, here's when I'll have a real update.* You don't apologise extensively. You don't explain at length. You name the thing, take responsibility for it, and demonstrate that the system that produced it is being corrected. Then you actually follow through.

This works because it does two jobs at once. It updates the model on the specific failure, which matters less than people think, and it confirms the model on the thing that matters more — that you'll surface failures publicly rather than hiding them. The second job is the bigger one. The team can absorb individual failures; they can't absorb the discovery that you'll let things slide quietly when nobody's watching.

The unrecoverable failures are the ones that confirm the team's prior bad model. Reversing your own commitments without naming it. Being more open with one team member than another and getting caught. Public correction of a decision someone has already made — especially one made in good faith, especially in a public forum. Escalating something after explicitly saying you wouldn't. Holding the team to standards you don't meet yourself. Not following up on things, repeatedly, in a pattern.

Each of these tells the team that the new manager is the old manager wearing a different face. The rebuild after one of these is much longer than after a single specific failure, because you're not updating the model on a specific event — you're trying to update the model on yourself, against weeks of contrary evidence the team has just collected.

A specific note on harsh feedback, because the instinct to deliver it is strongest in the moments when restraint matters most. Harsh treatment of someone who has missed the mark trades a correction for a delay. The recipient intended to do the right thing — almost everyone does — and instead of incorporating your feedback, they're now processing the harshness. Confidence drops. Work slows. The cost is paid in throughput for hours, sometimes days. The team also watches, and learns what happens when someone makes a mistake. Mistakes start getting hidden until they're too big to hide. The version that produces faster work is the same observation, asked rather than told. *I noticed X happened. What was going on?* Same content, different recovery curve. Chapter 1's *ask, don't tell* mantra is doing its operational job here — telling-harshly puts the recipient into a defensive posture from which they can't process correction effectively. Asking gives them a chance to see the problem and own the answer. Faster delivery comes from the second move, not the first.

The discipline isn't to be perfect. It's to be reliably truthful when imperfect, and to never slip into the kind of failure that confirms the team's worst model of management.

When the deficit predates you

Sometimes you walk into a team where the trust deficit predates you and you can't repair it on a normal timeline. The team has been burned by three previous managers, every one of whom said the right things in their first month. Your stated values mean nothing to them, because they've heard the same statement of values before, every time.

You do not try to short-circuit this.

You don't accelerate trust through workshops. You don't announce that things are going to be different. You don't tell the team you're "not like the previous person." All of these read as exactly what the previous person said, because the previous person did say them. Anything you assert about yourself becomes evidence against you.

What you do is operate predictably, deliver on small things, and let time do the work. The team's model of you will update on observed behaviour, which is a slow process and there is no shortcut. Three months in, they will start to notice that you've consistently done what you said you'd do. Six months in, the volunteer model will start to produce volunteers without you having to ask twice. Nine months in, the team will start raising concerns earlier rather than after they've become crises.

This is also when most managers leave. The honeymoon was over by month three, the team didn't seem to be improving, the manager started to feel ineffective, and the next role looked easier. The teams that get genuinely fixed have managers who stayed past the trust-rebuild floor. There's no way to know in month three whether you're on the right side of that timeline.

You just have to keep operating predictably and trust that the data will accumulate.

If you can't stay nine months, don't promise a transformation. Pick the smallest specific things you can credibly fix in the time you have, fix them, and leave the team in a slightly better state than you found it. That's also the lighter touch. Most managerial transformations fail because they were sized to the manager's ego rather than to the time the manager had.

Why the cheap fixes work

The book is built on cheap, observable, fast-acting fixes. Now you know why they work.

The fix to the standup isn't the format. It's that the team starts to trust that what they say in the standup will be acted on. Walk the board right to left, interrogate the cards that aren't moving, follow up on the blockers visibly — and within two weeks the team is using the standup to coordinate rather than to report up. The format change matters less than the trust signal embedded in it: when you raise a blocker, something happens.

The fix to the backlog isn't the structure. It's that the team starts to trust that the backlog reflects what will actually happen. Cull the dead tickets, mark unfunded items as "won't do," refine only what's near the top — and within a month the backlog stops being a graveyard and starts being a tool the team can plan around. Same trust mechanic. The signal that what's on the list is real changes how the team relates to the list.

The volunteer-leader model works because it's a trust signal made operational. So does open-by-default. So does the upstream-list visibility, the random-pick fallback, the no-half-measure rule. Every single move in chapters 1 and 2 is doing the same job: producing observable evidence that updates the team's model of you in the right direction.

Trust isn't the soft layer of the work. It's the operating principle the rest of the book sits on. The cheap fixes are cheap because the trust they build does the heavy lifting. The team's existing capability shows up once the system stops suppressing it. You're not adding new capability — you're removing the constraint that was hiding the capability you already had.

That's why the rest of the book is what it is. The ceremonies in Part 2 are the feedback loops that keep decision throughput honest. The cheap fixes in Part 3 are the moves that each, in their own way, repair a specific trust failure. Part 4 is what happens when AI removes one bottleneck and exposes the trust deficit underneath.

You now have the lens.

The rest of the book is the levers.

Part Two: The Ceremonies

The next eight chapters cover the recurring events of a team's working week — the one-on-one, the standup, planning, refinement, the retro, the demo, estimation, and the spike. Before taking them one at a time, this part needs one thing said about all of them, because it is the thing most teams have wrong. The trouble with a team's ceremonies is rarely how they are run. It is what the team believes they are.

Most teams run their ceremonies the way they were first taught them. Someone, once, showed them how a standup goes, and that is how the standup has gone ever since. The format hardened into a habit, the habit into a rule, and the rule into something nobody questions. Ask why the standup is run this way and the honest answer is usually "because that's how you do a standup." That is the moment a ceremony stops being a tool and becomes a ritual — performed because the calendar says so, in a shape nobody chose, with the original purpose long since worn away.

This is most of why "agile" has lost so much credibility. Not the ideas; the ideas are mostly sound. What discredited the word is a decade of teams performing the ceremonies without the thinking — standups that are status reports to a manager, retros that surface the same complaints every fortnight, planning that fills a sprint and calls that a plan. The motions, faithfully repeated, with the point missing. A team can do all of it, every event on schedule, and improve at nothing.

It is worth being honest about how an entire industry came to perform without thinking, because it was neither an accident nor stupidity. Agile began as a short, deliberately thin list of values, heavy on judgment. Then it was monetised — branded, certified, sold, with fortunes made teaching teams a way to be agile. There is nothing sinister in that by itself. But anything built to be sold has to be packaged, and judgment does not package. "It depends" cannot be examined at the end of a two-day course; a fixed sequence of events and roles can. So the part that scaled was the procedure, and the judgment that was the whole point of it was quietly left out of the box. A generation of teams was trained and certified on the steps of agile, and never taught the thinking those steps were there to serve.

The mistake underneath all of it is treating the framework as a rulebook. It isn't one. A framework is a frame, and a frame is mostly empty space. Scrum is the most prescriptive of the popular ones, and even Scrum really only specifies that certain feedback loops exist — that the team plans, syncs, reviews, and reflects on a regular cadence. It does not tell you what to think inside those loops. The prescription is the loops; everything that makes them worth running is supplied by the team.

This explains two complaints that sound like opposites and are really the same mistake. One team is sure it is "following the rules of agile"; another is sure the framework is too restrictive, broken, in need of adapting. Both have mistaken the frame for the picture. The first left the empty space blank and called the bare frame a finished work. The second felt the edges of the frame and blamed the frame. Neither noticed how little is actually there — to follow, or to resent.

Strip the branding off any of the popular frameworks and what remains is a small set of feedback loops — most of which the frameworks inherited, loosely, from the Toyota Production System. A feedback loop is not a cage. It cannot be too restrictive, because it restricts almost nothing; it cannot be broken, because there is barely anything in it to break; and it does not need adapting, because filling in the empty space was never a workaround for a faulty product — it is simply the work. What breaks, when a team's agile goes wrong, is the thinking the team was meant to bring to it.

So here is the frame worth holding for the whole of this part. A delivery team is a production system, and its ceremonies are the feedback loops that keep that system honest — each one a point where information comes in, a decision goes out, and the work moves. That is the only thing the ceremonies are for. A loop that takes in information and produces no decision is not a feedback loop. It is a meeting.

Most of these loops run with the whole team. Two do not, and they are worth naming up front because they bookend the rest. The one-on-one is the loop that runs one person at a time, in private — the place the team's quieter truths surface before they ever reach a room. The demo is the loop that runs with the people outside the team altogether — the place the work meets the judgement of whoever it is for. Between those two sit the loops the team runs on itself: the standup, planning, refinement, the retro, estimation, the spike. Private, collective, external — the same discipline runs through all of them. Information in, decision out, work moves.

The discipline that keeps those loops alive is worth a name: intentional work. Intentional work means nothing is picked up by reflex. You do not start a sprint because the last one ended — you plan it, with a clear picture of what done looks like. You do not pull a card because it is next — you pull it because it is genuinely ready, and you can say what result you are going out to get. At every step you are setting the bounds: what this is, what it is not, what would tell you it is finished. The opposite of intentional work is not laziness. It is sleepwalking — moving through the ceremonies competently, on time, and without ever quite deciding anything.

Intentional does not mean rigid, and it does not rule out exploration. A spike is intentional work too; the difference is only in what kind of result you go out for. Most work goes out to produce a finished thing. A spike goes out to produce a decision. Both are intentional. What is never intentional is picking up work without knowing which of the two you are doing.

Read the next eight chapters in that light. They are not a new set of rules to replace the rules you already had — that would just be a different ritual. They are eight feedback loops, and each chapter is about one question: how do you run this loop so that it takes in what it should and produces a decision worth having? The shape matters far less than that. A team that understands what a loop is for can run it in whatever form suits them and get the value. A team that has only learned the shape can run it perfectly and get nothing.

Chapter 4: One-on-Ones

A one-on-one is the only conversation in the working week that runs one person deep and stays private. That privacy is the whole point.

The rest of Part Two is about the team's public feedback loops — the standup, planning, refinement, the retro. All of those happen in the open, in a room with everyone in it. The one-on-one is the loop that runs underneath them, one person at a time, with the door shut. It exists to catch what the public loops can't.

What they can't catch is most of what's actually wrong.

A retro surfaces the problems a team is willing to say out loud, to each other, in front of whoever is in the room. That is a useful set of problems. It is not the whole set. The problems that don't surface in a retro — the senior engineer whose design decisions nobody will challenge, the dependency the team has quietly given up on, the suspicion that a stakeholder is acting in bad faith — are often the ones doing the most damage, precisely because they can't be said in public. The one-on-one is where they get said, or it is where nothing gets said and you find out too late.

Trust is the whole game

Before any of the technique, there is a precondition. Without it, you may as well not have a one-on-one. The precondition is trust.

Trust in this context means one specific thing: the person across from you believes that what they say will be received calmly, used carefully, and not turned against them. If they don't believe that, they will give you the sanitised version. They will tell you what they think you want to hear, flag the safe problems, and stay quiet about the ones that matter. And you will sit in one-on-ones every week believing you have an honest picture of the team, while the real picture stays hidden where you can't see it.

Trust is built through repeated small demonstrations. You tell someone you'll action something and you action it. You hear a difficult thing and your reaction is calm and constructive rather than defensive or punishing. You take a problem that was raised in confidence and you handle it in a way that protects the person who raised it. Every one of those moments either deposits into the account or withdraws from it.

The most important of these is how you react to bad news. When someone tells you something has gone wrong, or that a decision was a mistake, or that a colleague is struggling — your reaction in that moment is being memorised. Team members watch every reaction you have and build a model in their mind of how you will react. That model is what they consult before deciding whether to tell you something difficult. If you react badly, if you assign blame before you understand context, if you turn the information into a performance issue before you've heard the full story — you teach the whole team that honesty is costly. And the information stops flowing.

The real cost of that isn't the awkwardness of the one-on-one. It's what gets withheld at the moments you need it most. The problem that's been quietly growing for three weeks. The stakeholder who's been signalling something's wrong. The technical decision that's going sideways. The person who's about to leave. None of these surface to a manager who reacts badly to bad news. They arrive as surprises, long past the point when they were cheap to fix.

React calmly and pragmatically. Keep the focus on the work, not on the person. Ask what happened before you form a view on what should have happened. When you do that consistently, people start telling you the truth — and the truth is the only reason the meeting exists.

What you are actually there to catch

The obvious content of a one-on-one is the stuff you could get other ways. How is the person going. Are they stuck on anything. Have they spotted a problem with how the team works. That content is fine and you should cover it, but it is not the reason the meeting earns its place in the week.

The reason is leading indicators. A one-on-one is your earliest read on things that have not yet shown up on the board, in the metrics, or in a ceremony — and by the time they show up in those places, they have usually already cost you. Someone quietly losing faith in the direction. A tension between two people that is starting to slow their work. A decision everyone is treating as made that nobody actually made. These are not on any system. They live in people's heads, and the only way to reach them is to ask, one person at a time, and then listen.

The single most valuable thing you will work out from one-on-ones, over time, is who on the team drives change and who waits it out. Every team has both. The change-makers are the people who, when something is broken, want to fix it and will spend energy doing so. The others are content to roll with whatever happens — not malicious, not lazy, just not invested in improving the system around them. You need to know which is which, because the change-makers are who you build the rescue with. They are the ones who will carry a new way of running the standup when you are not in the room. The one-on-one is where you find them, because their instinct to improve things shows up in private long before it shows up in a meeting.

There is a tell worth noticing here, and it is slightly uncomfortable. Some people find one-on-ones close to useless — a box to tick, a half hour they would rather spend coding. In my experience that reaction correlates almost exactly with people who are not contributing to improving how the team works anyway. The person who finds the conversation valuable is usually the person with something they have been wanting to say. The person who finds it pointless usually has nothing they are trying to change. That is not a reason to cancel their one-on-one. It is a data point about where the team's improvement energy actually lives.

Cadence

Hold them regularly, and let the cadence follow the rate of change around the person.

Weekly if the environment is volatile — a new team, a troubled project, a reorganisation, anything where the ground is moving and a fortnight is long enough for a small problem to become a large one. Fortnightly if things are steady and the person is settled. The point of the cadence is to catch leading indicators while they are still leading. In a high-change environment, two weeks is enough time to miss the moment when something could have been cheaply fixed. In a steady one, weekly starts to feel like surveillance and you both run out of things to say, which trains the person to treat the meeting as theatre.

Adjust per person, not per policy. A blanket "everyone gets a weekly one-on-one" is easier to administer and worse in practice. The new starter who is still finding their feet needs more contact than the senior engineer who has been steady for two years. Match the cadence to the person and the moment.

Listen more than you talk

The discipline that makes or breaks the meeting is the ratio of listening to talking, and it should be heavily weighted toward listening.

This is harder than it sounds, because the manager's instinct is to fill the space — to update, to advise, to solve. Resist it. The value of the meeting is what you learn, and you learn nothing while you are talking. If you find yourself doing most of the talking in a one-on-one, the meeting has quietly become something else: a status briefing, a performance review, a venting session for you. None of those is the job.

Which leads to the single clearest rule about what a one-on-one is not. It is not a status update. Status — what got done, what's next, what's blocked — strips all the nuance out of the meeting and crowds out the things only this format can reach. And status belongs with the team anyway, in the open, where everyone can act on it. A blocker raised privately in a one-on-one is a blocker the rest of the team can't help with. Keep status in the standup and the board, and keep the one-on-one for what can't be said in public.

What surfaces here and nowhere else

The highest-value thing a one-on-one does is surface a problem that will never reach a retro — and then handle it without making the person who raised it pay for raising it.

When something is falling through the cracks of every ceremony, there is usually a reason, and the reason is usually one of two things. Either the team doesn't have enough psychological safety to say it out loud, or there is a political dimension that makes saying it costly. Someone is worried about how a senior person will react. Someone suspects a stakeholder of bad faith and can't prove it. Someone has noticed the emperor has no clothes and does not want to be the one to say so. These problems do not appear in the retro because the retro is public, and saying them in public carries a risk the person is not willing to take.

When you uncover one of these, your first move is to coach the person to raise it themselves. That is always the better outcome — a team where people can name the hard things in the open is a healthier team than one that routes everything through you. Give them the words. Help them see that the issue is about the work, not about a person, and that framing it that way makes it safe to say. Often that is enough.

But sometimes the lack of safety is real and the person genuinely cannot raise it without exposure they shouldn't have to bear. In that case, ask their permission to raise it yourself — and raise it anonymously. Strip the issue of every personal detail until what is left is the effect on the work. Not "Priya thinks the architecture is wrong and is scared to say so" but "I want us to look at how we're making technical decisions, because I think we might be building on assumptions we haven't tested." Depersonalise it completely and point it at the delivery. The goal is to get the problem onto the table without putting the person who raised it under a spotlight — because the moment they get burned for having spoken to you, every one-on-one you run after that becomes theatre.

Which is why the governing rule of one-on-ones is confidentiality. Everything said in a one-on-one stays in the one-on-one unless the person expressly tells you it can leave. Not "unless you think it's important." Not "unless it would help to share it." Unless they say so. The entire value of the format rests on people believing they can tell you the truth without it being used in a way they didn't sanction. Break that once, visibly, and you lose it with the whole team, because they talk to each other and word travels faster than any rescue you are trying to run.

Ask, don't tell

When you give feedback in a one-on-one, the form of the opening sentence decides whether the conversation works.

The instinct, when someone has made a mistake, is to tell them: *You made a mistake on those requirements. What are you going to do to improve?* It feels efficient and fair — you have named the problem and asked for a fix. It does not work, for two reasons.

The first is that you don't actually know what happened yet. You have seen the outcome, not the decision behind it. Without understanding the context — why the person did what they did, what they knew at the time, what pressure they were under — you cannot give feedback that is useful, because you are responding to the symptom and guessing at the cause. You might be about to coach them on a thing that wasn't the problem.

The second is what the opening does to the person. Lead with *you made a mistake* and you have started adversarially. Even if you are right, the person now feels bad, and feeling bad has a cost: their productivity and pace drop for a while as they replay the conversation and rebuild the confidence to get on with their work. You have created exactly the slowdown you were trying to prevent.

Now run the same conversation the other way. Open with a question: *How did you think it went with that requirement?* Most of the time you will get an honest admission that something wasn't right, and — more valuable — the root cause, in their own words. They were never briefed on the edge case. They flagged a risk that got waved off. They made a reasonable call on bad information. Now you know what actually happened, and you can follow up with the question that does the real work: *What do you think you'd need to do differently to stop that happening again?* When the person names the fix themselves, they own it. An action item someone arrives at on their own is one they will actually carry out. An action item you hand them is one they will resent and forget.

Coaching the individual

The last thing a one-on-one is good for is the coaching that doesn't apply to the whole team.

Some development is general — the kind of thing you'd run in a retro or a team session because everyone needs it. But some is specific to one person: a developer who is ready to start leading but doesn't see it yet, a quiet senior who should be mentoring and isn't, someone with the judgement to run a ceremony if you gave them the room. The one-on-one is where you do that work, because it is individual by nature and because the encouragement lands better in private than in front of the group.

These sessions, more than anything, are where you draw leadership behaviours out of people who have the capacity for them. The change-makers you identified earlier are the obvious candidates. A one-on-one is where you hand one of them a piece of the system to own — *you run refinement next sprint, I'll sit in the back* — and then coach them through it afterward. That is how a rescue outlives your involvement. The team that can run its own feedback loops well, without you in the room, is the team you have actually fixed. You build that team one one-on-one at a time.

The story that only came out one-on-one

I once inherited a team that could not get anything finished. The pattern looked like ordinary churn: the business analyst would meet the stakeholders, agree the functionality, get the requirements approved, and the team would build. Then at go-live the demo would surface edge cases and missing functionality, the stakeholders would object, and the cycle would restart. A fail loop with no exit.

I started, as always, with one-on-ones. One was unusually enlightening. A team member mentioned — in confidence, and nervous about it — that they'd heard from someone on the stakeholder side that the senior stakeholder driving the project had wanted, all along, to buy an off-the-shelf product rather than build one. Suddenly the fail loop made sense. The endless edge cases weren't a quality problem. The stakeholders didn't mind burning the team's time, because every failed go-live was evidence for the case the stakeholder actually wanted to make: that building this in-house was a mistake.

This is the kind of intelligence that never surfaces in a ceremony, and never will. It's political, it's sensitive, and the person carrying it has real reason to be nervous about sharing it. The only reason they shared it was because a few weeks of calm, consistent, confidential conversations had built enough trust that they were willing to take the risk. React badly to that disclosure

— or worse, let it slip who told you — and not only does that person never tell you anything important again, word gets around the team that the one-on-one door doesn't actually close.

I couldn't reveal the source, and I couldn't accuse anyone of anything I'd heard secondhand in confidence. What I could do was change the structure so the stakeholder had to commit instead of stall. The fail loop worked for him precisely because nothing was ever final — there was always another round, another edge case, more of the team's time to burn. So I removed the ability to stall. I had the team run sessions themed as "final requirements before we launch into production," and I told the senior stakeholders we'd completed the final round and were getting formal sign-off as the last gate before the first production launch — with the understanding that anything we discovered afterward could be remedied tactically once live, which internal apps allow.

The stakeholder signed off. About a day later the entire project was put on hold, and shortly after, axed. Forcing a real decision — making the stakes high and the moment unavoidable — had pushed him into the open. He couldn't keep the loop running once the next step was a launch he didn't actually want, so the real position finally surfaced. And the project landing in the bin was the right outcome. Building an off-the-shelf product inside an unsuitable low-code codebase, by five people typing it out by hand, never made business sense. The decision to kill it had been owed for months. All the sign-off gate did was collapse the decision debt that the fail loop had been hiding.

None of that was reachable from a ceremony. It was reachable because one person trusted the relationship enough to tell me something difficult, and because the conversation stayed confidential. That is the whole job of a one-on-one in one story.

Failure modes

Three patterns to watch for.

The one-on-one has become a status meeting. You spend the half hour going through what got done and what's next, and you both leave feeling it was efficient and slightly pointless. It was pointless, because all of that belonged in the standup and on the board. The fix is to ban status from the conversation and replace it with the questions only this format can ask: what is frustrating you that you haven't said, what would you change if it were your call, what's the thing you've been meaning to raise and haven't. If those questions produce nothing for several sessions running, that is itself a finding — either the person has genuinely nothing to improve, or they don't trust the meeting yet. Both tell you something.

You are doing most of the talking. You leave the one-on-one feeling good because you gave a lot of useful advice. The person leaves having learned that the meeting is for you, not them, and they stop bringing things. The fix is mechanical: count, roughly, who is talking. If it is mostly you, ask a question and then stay silent past the point of comfort. The thing they say after the silence is usually the thing worth the meeting.

Something said in confidence got out. You repeated a thing — to help, you told yourself — and the person it came from worked out that you had. This is the one failure you cannot walk back. Every one-on-one you run after it returns the sanitised version, because the team now knows the door doesn't actually shut. There is no fix, only prevention: confidential by default, always, and the anonymous-escalation move used only with explicit permission and the personal details genuinely stripped out.

The rescue, in week one

When you take over a team, one-on-ones are the first thing to set up, because they are how you build the map of who's who before you change anything.

In the first round, you are not there to fix or advise. You are there to listen and to learn the team. Ask each person the same few open questions — how do they think the team is going, what would they change if it were up to them, what's not working that nobody's saying — and then listen far more than you talk. Take the privacy seriously from the very first session, because the team is deciding, in those first conversations, whether you are someone they can tell the truth to.

By the end of the first round you will have something no ceremony would have given you: a read on where the change-makers are, where the blockers are, and at least one or two real problems that were never going to surface in a retro. That map is what you build the rest of the rescue on. The standup, the planning, the refinement, the retro — the next four chapters — all run better when you already know who in the room wants things to improve and who is waiting for you to leave.

The team's public feedback loops are where the work gets coordinated. The one-on-one is where you find out what the public loops can't tell you, and who is going to help you fix it. Start there.

Chapter 5: The Standup

THE standup is the ceremony most teams break first, and they break it in the most visible way. A meeting that was meant to coordinate today's work has turned into a status report to a manager — each person reciting what they did yesterday and will do today, to an audience of one who is the only person really listening. Everyone in the room can feel it's hollow. Nobody changes it, because changing it means admitting the daily ritual has been pointless for months.

This chapter is about turning it back into what it was for: a short, tactical session that produces a decision about today.

What a standup is for

A standup is a tactical session. Today's work, today's blockers, today's course-correction toward the goal. That's the job.

It is not a status report. It is not a daily check-in. It is not "communication." It is not an opportunity for the manager to know what each person is working on. Each of those framings is a different meeting, and each one — held at 9am with "standup" in the calendar invite — is what most teams have ended up with by accident.

The thing that makes a standup distinctive is that it's tied to the work. The team has a goal — a sprint goal, an iteration goal, a week's mission, whatever the label. The work in front of them either advances that goal or it doesn't. The standup is where the team decides, today, how to keep advancing it. Anything else that happens in the meeting is either useful (a tactical decision the work needs) or noise (everything else). The job is to get more of the first and less of the second.

Fifteen minutes is plenty for this when you're doing it right. Most teams take longer because they're not doing it right.

Walk the board, right to left

The single move that converts most broken standups into useful ones is the direction of the walk.

Most teams run their standup as a roll call. Each person speaks in turn. *Yesterday I worked on X, today I'll work on Y, no blockers.* The information transmitted is roughly zero — the team already had this from the board, the channel, and the PR queue — and the only person who learns anything is the manager, who doesn't usually need to.

The alternative is to walk the board instead of the people. Start at the rightmost column where work is closest to done, and move left. For each card: what does this need to finish? Who's doing the next move? Anything blocking? Anything that means this card shouldn't be on the board today at all?

The right-to-left direction matters. Left-to-right starts with the work the team hasn't begun yet — which is the work that's easiest to feel productive about, and the work the team should mostly not be touching while there's still incomplete work to the right. Right-to-left starts with the work closest to done — which is the work that needs to actually be finished before anyone picks up anything new. The board's nervous system runs in this direction. The standup that walks it in this direction respects that.

There's a deeper reason. Right-to-left is pull, not push. You're closing work before starting new work. A team that walks left-to-right naturally accumulates WIP, because every standup is an opportunity to start something. A team that walks right-to-left naturally drains it, because every standup is an opportunity to finish something. Same fifteen minutes; opposite direction; opposite outcome.

For each card you walk, the question is the same. What is this card waiting on? If the answer is "nothing, it's just being worked on," skip it. If the answer is "the reviewer," that's a tactical conversation the standup can have. If the answer is "I'm not sure what done looks like," the card is in the wrong place — it shouldn't be in progress, it should be back at refinement. The standup is where you catch this.

What goes async

Most of what happens in a status standup belongs in async.

"Yesterday I worked on the auth refactor" is a status update. It goes in the ticket, the channel, the standup bot if the team uses one. Not in the meeting. The team that needs this information has it already; the team that doesn't, doesn't need to spend two minutes per person learning it.

"Today I'll work on the auth refactor" is also a status update. Also async.

"I'm blocked on the API spec" is borderline. If the API spec is going to get unblocked by someone in the room, it's a tactical conversation worth having. If it's going to require a separate call with a different team, it's a status update that ends with "and here's what I'm doing about it."

The principle is: the meeting holds what requires synchronisation. Coordination conversations. Blocker resolution where the resolver is in the room. Tactical decisions that need to happen now because the work needs them today. Everything else goes async.

A consequence of this is that people who don't have anything to add don't have to speak. The default isn't "everyone speaks once around the circle." The default is silence broken only by what the work needs. A junior developer who's heads-down on a card that's progressing fine doesn't have to perform an update. A senior developer who finished their card yesterday and is starting the next thing doesn't have to announce it. The board shows what they're doing. The standup shows what needs the team's attention.

This is uncomfortable for teams who've been trained that the standup is where you prove you're working. They feel awkward saying nothing. The fix is to keep doing the right-to-left walk and let them experience that nothing bad happens when they don't speak. Two weeks of that and the awkwardness stops.

Don't wait for standup

A standup is a synchronisation point, not a queue. The meeting tomorrow at 9am isn't where you raise the blocker you discovered at 10am today. You raise it now, in whatever channel will get it resolved fastest. The standup is what's left over after everything urgent has already been raised.

This sounds obvious and it isn't, because most teams have built up an unspoken rule that "issues" are what you raise at standup. The result is that blockers wait twelve, twenty, sometimes twenty-four hours to surface — and the work behind them sits idle in the meantime. The standup becomes a queue of things the team has been politely sitting on overnight rather than acting on immediately. Each blocker raised at standup is, on average, half a day of slowed work that didn't have to happen.

The rule is: if it's urgent, raise it now. The team channel, a direct message to whoever can unblock, a quick walk over to a desk, whatever moves fastest. Save the standup for things that genuinely need synchronisation across the team and aren't urgent enough to interrupt anyone immediately — course-correction conversations, the "anyone got bandwidth to pair on this gnarly card today" question, the "we need to swap who's reviewing what" conversation. Things where everyone's awareness matters and the cost of waiting half a day is small.

The signal that the rule isn't taking is a standup that surfaces yesterday's blockers. If someone says "I've been blocked on the API spec since yesterday afternoon" at 9am the next day, the team has a habit problem — something stopped them from raising it twenty hours ago. The fix is to ask, openly, what stopped them. Usually it's the unspoken rule that issues belong at standup. Once that's named, it goes away.

The goal as the anchor

The walk has to be tied to a goal. Without one, every card looks equally important and the standup degrades into a tour of activity.

The goal is what makes "is this card progressing the work?" a real question. Sprint goal, iteration outcome, week's mission — the label matters less than the existence. If the team can't articulate what they're trying to achieve this sprint in one sentence, the standup is going to drift, because there's no anchor for deciding what matters today.

Two operational moves come from this.

First, the standup is where you catch cards that aren't serving the goal. Not every card on the board is goal-aligned — there will always be some support work, some carryover, some "just one more thing" that snuck in. Some of that's fine. But when the goal is at risk, cards that don't serve it should come off the board, and the standup is where the team makes that call. *We're going to drop the dashboard refresh card this sprint — it's not blocking the goal and it's pulling capacity away.* Goal-anchored standups make this conversation small. Goalless standups make it impossible.

Second, the standup is where the team course-corrects. If yesterday's plan no longer matches today's reality — someone's out sick, a card got harder than expected, a stakeholder changed direction — the team adjusts the plan in the meeting. Not by re-running planning. Just by saying *here's what changed; here's how we're going to respond.* The plan was always a hypothesis, and the standup is where the hypothesis meets reality.

A team without a goal can't do either of these. They run a tour of activity, learn nothing, leave, and discover at the end of the sprint that the work added up to less than they thought. The fix isn't a better standup. It's a goal. Which is the next chapter.

Tactical decisions, not displaced ones

Decisions get made in good standups. They have to — the meeting wouldn't be useful otherwise. But there's a kind of decision a standup is for and a kind it isn't.

The right kind are tactical. Who's pairing on the gnarly card today. Who's covering on-call while someone's at a customer meeting. What gets dropped because capacity has shifted. Whether to let the senior developer focus on review for the morning to clear the queue. These decisions need to happen now, they need to happen with everyone present, and they need to happen quickly. The standup is the right forum.

The wrong kind are displaced. Architectural arguments. Scope changes. Prioritisation calls about which feature matters more. These decisions either belong in another ceremony — refinement, planning, a design conversation — or they belong async, with the right people present and the time to think. When they happen in standup, two things go wrong. The decision is made worse, because it's rushed and the right people might not all be in the room. And the standup balloons, because the conversation eats fifteen minutes that should have been five.

The five-minute rule is the discipline. If a conversation in the standup looks like it's going to run longer than five minutes, it gets parked. *Let's pick this up after the standup with the people who need to be in it.* Then the standup keeps moving. Three or four parked items in a single standup is a sign the team has been making decisions in the meeting that should have been made elsewhere — which is a chapter 1 diagnostic signal you're now picking up by running the rescue.

When the walk reveals more than expected

I had a team once where the product manager objected to the right-to-left walk on day two. *We don't actually need to do this, half the cards are blocked anyway, this is a waste of time.* He wanted the standup to skim the board and end fast. The team wanted to keep walking. They walked it.

The cards were blocked on client testing. Tickets sat in a "blocked" column waiting for the customer to validate. Some had been there four weeks. The team had got used to it — the column had become a kind of waiting room they'd stopped visiting. Walking the board meant standing in that room every morning and naming each card that hadn't moved. *Still blocked. Still blocked. Still blocked. Still blocked.* It was painful, and the pain was the point.

We did it for three more days. Each morning the team had to confront the same dead cards by name. By the third day the conversation shifted from *"yes, still blocked"* to *"why is this still blocked, and what would it take to actually finish it or kill it?"* That's the conversation the team had been avoiding for a month, because the column had let them avoid it. And once the team started asking, the answer surfaced fast. The clients weren't slow to test; they were unprepared to test. Onboarding hadn't finished. They hadn't been set up correctly. The PM was responsible for that front-end work. The cards stacking up at the right of the board were the visible consequence of his upstream work being incomplete. That's why he didn't want the walk. The walk made his unfinished work into the team's problem.

The fix wasn't to move the cards somewhere off the board. It was to send them back to To Do. The team made the call that work wasn't ready to be picked up until a client testing slot was actually scheduled. No scheduled testing time, no pull into progress. The cards stopped being mid-flight inventory and went back to being unstarted work — which is what they actually were. They didn't disappear; they just stopped pretending to flow when they weren't flowing. The team stayed in active communication with clients to schedule testing windows, and when a slot was confirmed, the card got pulled into progress with a real path to done.

Two patterns generalise out of that one situation, and they're both the chapter's job to name.

The first is the principle the team's resolution embodies. Work doesn't begin until the conditions for it to finish are real. A card without a scheduled finish isn't in progress, it's queued. Treating queued work as in-progress work is what creates the blocked-column theatre — the cards aren't moving, but the team has visually committed to them, so they sit. Sending them back to To Do isn't admitting failure. It's correcting a mis-categorisation. The work hadn't started; the team had just been pretending it had. Once the rule is clear — *no scheduled finish, no pull* — the board starts showing what the team is actually doing, and the actual in-progress work is usually much smaller than the team thought. They can see flow again because there is flow to see.

The instinct in this situation is to fix the board format — add a "waiting on customer" swim lane, colour-code the stalled cards, build a Kanban board with custom columns. Resist that. The fix isn't a richer board. The fix is a stricter rule about what counts as in progress. One status, one meaning. Don't let the team commit visually to work that hasn't actually started.

The second pattern is about who resists the walk and why. Downstream pile-ups reveal upstream failures. The work flowing through your team stops at the same place every time, and the same place is usually downstream of where the actual problem lives. The walk doesn't just surface the bottleneck — it traces the bottleneck back to its source. The people most likely to object to the walk are sometimes the people whose upstream work is creating the pile-up. They usually aren't doing it consciously. They genuinely think the walk is wasting time, because the cards waiting on something they own feel like background noise from where they're sitting. The walk reframes the noise as inventory, and inventory has a name on it. Once it does, it stops being easy to ignore.

You don't argue with the objection. You keep walking the board, and you let the work being stuck become something the team can see together. The conversation that follows is the rescue. Not the meeting format. The meeting making the system legible to the people inside it.

The rescue, in week one

Most readers of this chapter have a status standup, not a tactical one. The conversion is straightforward but specific.

In your first standup as the person running it: don't run it as a roll call. Walk the board. Start at the rightmost column. For each card, ask the questions — what does this need to finish, anyone blocking, is this still on the goal. Most of the team will be confused for the first minute, because the format has changed and they were preparing their roll-call answer. The confusion passes.

Set the expectation explicitly: people don't have to speak unless the work needs them to. *We're going to walk the board today. If you've got something the team needs to know, raise it. If you don't, that's fine.* The first time someone notices they haven't spoken and panics, the rescue is taking. The first time someone says "I don't have anything for the team today" and the standup moves on without them being singled out, the team has learned the new shape.

When a conversation runs long, park it. *That's a longer conversation than the standup can hold. Let's pick it up after with [the right people].* Then move on. The first time you do this someone will be irritated; the second time, the team will start parking things on their own.

After the standup, watch what happens. Do the parked items actually get picked up? Do the named tactical decisions get acted on? Do the blockers get unblocked? If yes, the meeting is doing its job. If not, the format change hasn't taken — the team has migrated from one kind of theatre to another.

Within two weeks the standup is either revealing where decisions are stuck (the meeting is doing its job) or revealing that the team has very little to coordinate (which is itself diagnostic). Both outcomes are useful. The third outcome — the standup runs faster but the work doesn't move — means the rescue hasn't taken and you're in failure-mode territory.

Failure modes

Three patterns to watch for after the rescue. Each has a specific corrective.

The standup got shorter but the work didn't move. The team migrated the status-report theatre to async without picking up the coordination habit. They walk the board, say nothing, leave, and the same blockers persist. The fix is to slow down on specific cards rather than speeding through all of them. When you hit a card that hasn't moved in three days, stop. Make the conversation happen now. *This card has been here for three days — what does it need?* The team will resist this because it feels like singling out, but the discomfort is the rescue working: the team is being forced to coordinate on the work the meeting was supposed to coordinate on all along.

One person dominates the right-to-left walk. Usually a senior developer or tech lead who's taken on the role of narrating each card. You've replaced the boss-status-report with the senior-engineer-status-report. The fix is to ask the question to the room, not to a person. *This card — what does it need?* If only one person ever answers, you have a different problem — and it's worth being honest about which one. Sometimes it's a trust problem (the team isn't engaging with each other's work, which is chapter 3). But often it's a goal problem: only one person is bought into what the sprint is for, so only one person is doing the work of asking whether each card is serving it. Everyone else is along for the ride. The standup format isn't going to fix either version on its own. If the goal isn't shared, the next chapter is where the rescue starts — you re-run planning so the goal is something the whole team owns, not something that's been handed to them.

The team starts skipping the standup. Cancellations, late starts, half the team absent. This is the most worrying pattern, because it means the standup isn't doing enough work to justify the time. Two possibilities. Either the team genuinely has very little to coordinate — in which case standup three days a week is fine, every day is overkill, and the meeting was always doing less than people thought. Or the team has decided the standup isn't worth their time, in which case something about the new format isn't landing and you need a one-on-one to find out what.

The standup, like every ceremony in this part, is an instrument. If the instrument isn't reading, you check the instrument. You don't keep running the meeting and pretending it's fine.

The next chapter is about planning — the ceremony where the goal that anchors every standup gets set, contested, and committed to. If the standup is where you check whether today's work is still serving the goal, planning is where you make sure there's a goal worth serving in the first place.

Chapter 6: Planning

A planning session is where the team turns a goal into a plan.

It is not a ceremony for moving cards from the backlog into the sprint. It is not a forecasting exercise. It is not "choosing what to commit to" in the way most teams treat it — pulling tickets off the top of the queue until someone says "that feels about right." Each of those is a different thing, and each one held at 10am with "sprint planning" in the calendar invite is what most teams have ended up with by accident.

The thing that makes planning distinctive is the direction it runs. Good planning starts with the goal and builds toward the work. Bad planning starts with the work and hopes a goal will emerge. Most teams do the second and call it the first. This chapter is about how to actually do the first.

Goal first, not backlog first

Open the backlog at the start of planning and you've already lost.

The reason is structural. The backlog is the accumulation of every decision the team and its stakeholders have ever made about what might be worth doing. It contains good ideas and stale ideas, urgent items and items that have been deferred for two years because nobody has the heart to close them. Pulling the top items off this pile and calling the result a sprint isn't planning — it's archaeology with a deadline. The team ends up with a list of cards that may or may not add up to anything, because they were never selected to add up to anything.

The inversion is to start with the goal. *What are we trying to achieve in the next two weeks?* That question gets answered first, before anyone touches the backlog. The goal is the unit of planning, not the cards. Once the goal is clear, the work that achieves it gets identified — and only then does the backlog come into the conversation, as one of several places that work might already exist.

This sounds like a small change of order. It isn't. The two approaches produce structurally different sprints.

Cards-first planning produces a sprint backlog. Goal-first planning produces an execution plan. A sprint backlog is a list of tickets the team has agreed to attempt. An execution plan is a goal at the top, the work that achieves it underneath, and a sequencing that gives the team a path. The first artefact tells the team what to do next. The second tells the team what they're trying to do, what would have to be true for them to do it, and how they're going to do it.

The team that walks out of planning with a sprint backlog has agreed to a list of tasks. The team that walks out of planning with an execution plan has agreed to a destination. When the sprint hits something unexpected — and it will — the first team has to re-plan. The second team can adjust without losing direction, because the goal is still there.

What an execution plan actually contains

An execution plan has three kinds of work in it, and recognising the distinction is what makes the inversion practical.

The first kind is **existing cards from the backlog that serve the goal**. Most goals will pull at least some work that's already been refined and is sitting in the backlog ready to go. This is what most teams already know how to do — open the backlog, pick the cards that serve the goal, drag them into the sprint. The change is that you're picking cards because they serve the goal, not because they're at the top of the backlog. Most cards at the top of the backlog *don't* serve a particular goal — they're just the most recent additions, or the highest-priority items in some abstract sense. Goal-first planning is selective in a way backlog-first planning isn't.

The second kind is **new cards for work the backlog didn't have**. Almost every goal-first plan reveals work the backlog hadn't captured. Sometimes that's a coordination piece — a conversation with another team, a decision that hasn't been made yet, a dependency that needs to be confirmed. Sometimes it's an integration step that was implicit in someone's head and hadn't been written down. Sometimes it's just a bit of work that fell through the cracks. New cards get created during planning, refined just enough to be actionable, and added to the plan. This is normal. The backlog is never going to be a complete map of the work.

The third kind is **checklist items inside the plan that don't deserve their own card**. Some work needs to happen but doesn't need to be tracked separately. *Get the database credentials from infra. Confirm the staging environment is current. Send a heads-up to the support team about the rollout window.* These are real steps. They take time. If they don't happen, the goal slips. But each one is small enough that giving it a Jira ticket would be more bureaucratic than useful — the ceremony of creating, refining, picking up, working, and closing a ticket would take longer than the work itself. Putting them on the plan as checklist items makes them visible without making them bureaucratic.

The output of planning is all three together. A goal at the top. The cards that serve it (existing and new). The checklist items that need to happen alongside the cards. A sequencing that says what depends on what. That's an execution plan. That's what the team should walk out of planning with.

The goal has to be the team's

A goal that one person constructs and the rest of the team acknowledges isn't a goal. It's a briefing.

This is where the chapter on trust pays into the chapter on planning. Chapter 3 made the case that the team trusts you when they can predict what you'll do, and you trust the team when you stop checking on what you've delegated. Planning is one of the highest-leverage tests of both directions. If the team trusts the goal, they'll defend it under pressure. If they don't, they'll abandon it the moment the sprint gets hard. The standup will tell you which version you have.

The test is simple. After planning, ask each team member separately: *what are we trying to achieve this sprint?* If you get three different answers in three different words but the same underlying intent, the goal is shared. If you get three different intents — or worse, the same recited phrase from each person, delivered without conviction — the goal hasn't formed. Acknowledgment isn't ownership.

A team that can't articulate its goal isn't just failing at internal coordination — it's also drifting from what the company is trying to achieve. The goal is the team's bridge between strategy upstream and stakeholder communication downstream. From inside the team, the goal feels implicit in the cards. From the outside — to leadership, stakeholders, the rest of the company — the cards are just activity. The team is flat out, and stakeholders think they're doing nothing, because nobody can name what's being delivered. *We're shipping the integration with X this sprint* is legible. *We're working through the integration backlog* isn't. The goal isn't bureaucratic overhead. It's how the team stays anchored to what matters and how it shows that work to the people who decide whether the team continues to exist. Without that anchoring, even hard-working teams drift — locally optimised, strategically adrift, slowly losing the recognition and trust they need.

Constructing a shared goal in planning is operationally specific. Don't arrive with the goal pre-formed. Arrive with the inputs — what leadership has asked for, what users need, what the team has been working on, what the previous sprint did or didn't deliver — and let the team synthesise. The synthesis is the work. If you've already synthesised it before the meeting, you've reduced planning to a briefing dressed up as collaboration.

This will feel slow the first few times. A team that's used to being handed a goal will look at you blankly when you ask them to construct one. *Isn't that your job?* It isn't. The goal is the team's by construction or it isn't really the team's at all. Sit with the slowness. The first few planning sessions where the team builds the goal themselves will feel inefficient. The sprints that follow will be measurably better, because the team is now defending something they own rather than executing something they've been given.

If the team pushes back on a proposed goal — *we don't think this is achievable in two weeks, we don't think this is the right priority, we don't have the people to do this* — take it seriously. Pushback is the team showing you their understanding of the work. The wrong response is to overrule the pushback because leadership wants what they want. The right response is to surface the push-back to the level where it can be properly addressed. *The team is telling me this isn't achievable in the time we have. Do we want to change the goal, change the timeline, or change what's in scope?* That's a real planning conversation. Forcing the goal through over the team's objections produces a sprint backlog with a goal printed at the top, not an execution plan.

Who needs to be in the room

Planning fails when the decisions can't be made.

This sounds like a different problem than goal-setting or work-identification, but it's the same problem expressed differently. The team can't commit to a goal if the person who decides what the goal is isn't there. The team can't sequence the work if the person who has to do half of it works on a different team and hasn't been invited. The team can't agree to a date if the dependency owner hasn't said whether they'll deliver in time.

The rule is straightforward: anyone whose decision the plan depends on needs to be in the room. The product manager who'll set scope. The tech lead or architect who can call which approach is viable. The team that owns the upstream API the work depends on, if you're relying on them to ship. The stakeholder who'll sign off on the deliverable, if their sign-off is on the critical path.

This is uncomfortable because the standard advice is that planning is the team's meeting, and inviting outsiders dilutes the team's ownership. The standard advice is wrong on this. Planning is the meeting where the team turns a goal into a plan. If half the plan depends on people outside the team, those people need to be at planning, or the plan is fiction. Pretending the team can plan in isolation when they can't doesn't preserve their ownership — it just produces an execution plan that can't actually be executed.

There's a softer version that works: dependencies don't need to attend the whole meeting, just the part where their commitment matters. Block off the first thirty minutes for cross-team alignment, then run the rest of planning with just the team. That's usually a reasonable compromise. The non-compromise is letting planning produce commitments from people who weren't there.

The signal that this rule isn't taking is the phrase *"we'll need to check with [other team]"* appearing in planning. Every time it comes up, the team has just made a planning assumption based on guesswork rather than commitment. That's risk being added to the plan that nobody is owning.

WIP zero between sprints

If the previous sprint succeeded, there is nothing in progress at the start of the next planning session.

This is the rule most teams break the most consistently, and the breakage is one of the largest sources of slow delivery in software. The pattern is familiar. Sprint ends Friday. Three cards didn't quite finish — the PR is in review, the tests are flaky, the deploy is waiting on a window. The team rolls them into next sprint. Adds a few more cards. Calls it planning. Repeats.

The cost compounds. Each rolled-over card is a context switch the team has to pay for again — by the time someone goes back to it, they've forgotten the details and have to rebuild context that was warm two weeks ago. The cards added to the new sprint land in a system that's already partially loaded, so they get less attention than they should. The goal of the new sprint is contaminated by carry-over from the old one, and the team's capacity to commit is overstated because they're effectively starting at WIP > 0. Multiply this across six months and the team is in a permanent state of half-finished work, never starting clean, never closing clean.

The discipline is to enforce the gap. If the previous sprint succeeded, WIP is zero between sprints — the cards either finished or they got pulled out of scope and are no longer the team's problem until they're explicitly reintroduced. If the previous sprint didn't succeed, the rolled-over work isn't quietly absorbed into the next sprint; it's named, examined, and decided on. *We didn't finish the auth refactor. Why? What changed? Are we going to finish it next sprint, or are we going to acknowledge it didn't fit and re-plan accordingly?* That conversation is the retro's job, partly, but the planning that follows it has to honour what the retro found. Quietly carrying work forward makes the retro irrelevant — the team has already absorbed the failure into the next sprint without learning from it.

There's a softer version of this rule that's defensible: *carry-over needs to be visible and decided, not automatic.* If the team finishes a sprint with one card in review that will close on Monday, fine — note it, plan around it, move on. The problem isn't that some work occasionally crosses the boundary. The problem is the *default* of carrying work over without examining whether the previous sprint actually succeeded. Each rolled-over card needs to be a decision the team made deliberately, not an inheritance the team accepted by inertia.

When goal-setting reveals more than expected

I joined a team once that had a textbook planning problem. Five engineers, one PM, building a B2B integrations product. Sprints "succeeded" — the team usually closed about 80% of the cards they took on — but nothing they shipped felt like it added up. Customers were asking for the same things they'd asked for six months earlier. The PM was frustrated. The team was working hard. None of them could quite say what they were trying to achieve.

I attended my first planning session as the new DM, expecting to mostly observe. The PM opened by sharing his screen with a list of cards. Twelve of them, ordered by his sense of priority. The team started estimating. A senior engineer pushed back on one that looked too big. They swapped it out. The conversation drifted into a debate about whether two of the cards were actually related. Nobody had said anything about what the sprint was for.

I stopped them. *Quick question before we keep going. What's the goal of this sprint?*

A senior engineer pushed back. *Isn't it obvious? It's the cards we're working on.*

I can see you're all doing a ton of work, I said, *but none of it is being recognised because there's no coherent goal we can report progress on. Stakeholders think the team is doing nothing but you're all flat out busy.*

Someone — predictably — said *yeah, well, they don't understand what we do.*

Then we need to communicate with them in a way that's transparent and looks like we're working towards the company's goals. Which we can't do if we can't say what our goal is.

The PM tried: *well, the cards we just talked about* — which isn't a goal, it's a list. I tried again. *What's the number one priority for the team this sprint? If we could only ship one thing, what would it be?*

Crickets. Five engineers and a PM, all looking at their laptops. After ten seconds someone offered *the integration with X, I guess?* — but it was a question, not a statement.

That's when I knew the planning had been broken for a while. The team hadn't just lost the ability to pick a goal — their work had drifted from anything the company was actually trying to achieve. The cards on the screen made sense individually but didn't add up to a contribution the business needed. The lost ability to articulate a goal was the symptom. The disconnection from the company's strategy was the cause.

I offered an alternative. *Let's not pick cards today. Let's start somewhere else. What would have to be true at the end of two weeks for this sprint to feel like it succeeded?* The PM was uncomfortable — *we've got a lot to get through* — but the team was curious, and the curiosity won. We spent the next forty minutes trying to articulate one outcome the sprint would aim for. Eventually the PM landed it: *we'd have one customer using the new integration end-to-end in production.* The team agreed. That was the goal.

Then we identified the work. Some of it was already in the backlog, refined and ready. Some was new — a coordination piece with another product team, a configuration step we'd missed, a customer-comms task that was implicit but uncaptured. Some was checklist items inside the plan that didn't deserve cards: confirm the rollback plan, schedule the go-live window with the customer, get the staging credentials.

About an hour in, we hit the wall. Half the work depended on a deployment change that devops owned, and nobody on our team could speak for them. I paused the session. *We can't finish planning today. We need someone from devops here, and probably from the customer-comms team too. Let's reconvene tomorrow morning, and I'll get them on the call for the first thirty minutes.* The PM was visibly uncomfortable. *We've never split planning across two days.* I held the line. The alternative was walking out with a plan that depended on commitments we couldn't make.

The devops lead and a customer-comms manager joined the next morning. We spent thirty minutes confirming what they could deliver and when. Devops could ship the deployment change by Wednesday — too late for our original sequencing, but workable if we reordered the work. Customer-comms agreed to schedule the go-live with us instead of being told about it after the fact. We rebuilt the plan around those commitments. The team walked out with a goal, a sequenced execution plan, and real buy-in from the dependencies. The whole exercise took about two hours over two days.

The sprint succeeded — not in the *closed 80% of cards* sense, but in the *one customer using the new integration end-to-end in production* sense. That had been the goal. That's what was true at the end. The previous sprints had succeeded by their own measure too, but their measure had been the cards, not the outcome.

The junior dev said something at the next retro that mattered. *I've been working through this backlog for two years. I've never once actually achieved a customer goal in a single sprint. It feels good to actually ship something in a sprint.* The PM agreed that he had lost control of the goals a while back becoming overwhelmed with support tickets and constant changes in direction from leadership. That was the shift. They stopped arriving at planning sessions with a bunch of cards at the top of the backlog. They started arriving with a mandate.

The lesson generalises beyond the specific situation. The team had been "successful" by the metric that was easiest to measure — cards closed — and unsuccessful by the metric that mattered: whether the work added up to anything the company was trying to achieve. Goal-first planning forces that question into the conversation. Backlog-first planning never asks it. The team doesn't know what they're trying to achieve, so neither does anyone else.

When one session isn't enough

Planning is a tool, not a ritual. If sixty minutes leaves the team with fuzzy alignment, run another thirty.

This is the rule the chapter is going to push back on the orthodox view to defend. Most agile texts treat planning as a fixed-length event — two hours per sprint week, run once at the start of each sprint, done. The implicit assumption is that the team will arrive at clarity in that window or fake it. Faking it is what most teams do, because the alternative — sitting in the room and admitting the goal isn't clear yet — feels like the meeting failing.

It isn't the meeting failing. The meeting failing is leaving the room with a sprint backlog the team doesn't believe in. Running an extra thirty minutes — or scheduling a follow-up the next morning — to actually nail down the goal is the meeting succeeding at its job. The orthodoxy that planning is one fixed event held once per sprint is framework-worship. Reality is that planning takes as long as it takes for the team to walk out with a real plan, and the alternative — under-planned sprints producing wrong-thing-built waste — is far more expensive than another half-hour in a room.

The signals that you need a second session: the team agreed in the room but the conversation since has revealed that "agreement" was different things to different people. New information surfaced after the meeting that changes the plan. Someone who needed to be there wasn't, and what they would have said matters. Any of those is enough. Schedule the follow-up. Don't pretend the first session got the job done.

What you don't do is let planning sprawl indefinitely. A team that consistently needs three sessions per sprint to plan has a different problem — usually that the goal-setting work isn't happening upstream of planning, so planning is doing double duty. The fix isn't more planning sessions, it's making sure the goal-shaping work happens earlier — through one-on-ones with leadership, async conversations with the team, refinement work that surfaces the questions before they hit planning. Planning should be where the team converts a roughly-known goal into a concrete plan, not where the goal itself gets discovered for the first time.

Failure modes

Three patterns to watch for after the rescue. Each one tells you something specific about why planning isn't producing what it should.

The team walks out with a sprint backlog, not a plan. Cards got picked, capacity got matched, calendars got blocked. But ask the team afterward what they're trying to achieve and you get five different answers, or worse, the answer is just a list of the cards. The goal didn't form. The team has agreed to a list of work, not a destination. The fix is to refuse to end the planning session until the goal can be articulated by every team member in their own words. *Before we close, can each of us say what we're trying to achieve this sprint?* If three of the five answers are "ship the cards we just talked about," the meeting hasn't done its job and you need another session.

The goal was handed to the team, not constructed with them. This usually shows up in the first sprint after a leadership change, or after a quarterly planning event where someone above the team has decided what the team's priorities are. The goal is real — leadership wants what they want — but the team hasn't owned it. They'll execute on it dutifully and the sprint will probably even succeed, but the team's commitment is shallow. The standup will reflect this — only one or two people engage with whether the work is serving the goal, because only one or two people are actually committed to it. The fix isn't to override leadership; it's to translate. Sit with the team and ask *what does this look like for us — what do we need to believe about this goal to commit to it?* The translation work makes the goal theirs, even when the goal originated elsewhere. Without that translation, planning produces compliance, not commitment.

Carry-over has become invisible. Each sprint starts at WIP > 0 and nobody notices. The team has trained itself to absorb whatever didn't finish into the next sprint, and the planning session has become a ritual of stacking new work on top of unfinished work. The fix is uncomfortable: name what's carrying over, in the planning session, every time. *We're starting this sprint with three cards from last sprint still open. Before we add anything new, what are we doing about those three?* The team will resist this because it feels like dragging up old failure, but the resistance is the point. A planning session that doesn't surface what didn't finish is a planning session that has lost the ability to learn from what didn't work.

The rescue, in week one

Most teams you'll inherit run planning backlog-first. The conversion to goal-first is straightforward but specific.

In your first planning session: don't open the backlog. Don't even put it on the screen. Open the meeting with the goal question. *What are we trying to achieve this sprint?* If the team has a goal in mind, sharpen it. If they don't, refuse to plan until they do. Sit with the silence if the silence comes. The discomfort of a team realising they don't have a goal yet is the rescue working — the meeting is forcing the work that was previously being skipped.

Once the goal is clear, ask the team to identify the work that would achieve it. Existing cards from the backlog get pulled in. New cards get created for work the backlog didn't have. Discrete steps that don't deserve cards go into a checklist. The output is the plan. Sequencing comes last — what depends on what, what has to be done before what, who's likely to lead which piece. Sixty to ninety minutes is reasonable for the first session. Subsequent sessions, with the team trained, will run shorter.

End the session with the test: *can each of us say what we're trying to achieve this sprint?* Go around the room. If the answers converge, the goal is shared and planning is done. If they don't, schedule the follow-up before everyone leaves. Don't pretend the meeting got the job done when the test failed.

In the standups that follow, you'll see whether the rescue took. A team operating from a real goal walks the board with the question *is this still serving the goal?* in mind. A team operating from a sprint backlog walks the board card by card, asking *is this card progressing.* Same walk, different question. The first one produces course-correction; the second one produces a slightly more efficient version of the wrong thing.

The next chapter is about refinement — the ceremony where cards get made ready to pull. Planning takes a goal and finds the work that achieves it. Refinement takes the work and makes it ready to be done. Without refinement, planning has nothing to draw on; without planning, refinement is just churning through cards that may or may not matter.

Chapter 7: Refinement

REFINEMENT is where the team decides what work actually means before building it.

Not writes it down. Decides it. The writing follows the decision. A team that leaves refinement with beautiful user stories but no shared understanding has not refined anything. A team that leaves with rough notes and a sketch but everyone at the table knows exactly what they're building has done the job. The ticket is not the point of refinement. The shared understanding is the point. The ticket is just a record of the conversation that happened.

Most teams treat refinement as a writing exercise. They're trying to get the ticket right — more acceptance criteria, cleaner user story format, better edge-case coverage. Some of that matters, but it's the wrong frame for the job. You can write a perfect ticket that nobody understands, and you can write a three-sentence ticket that the whole team can build from memory. The difference isn't the writing. It's whether the decision was made in the room.

What "ready to build" actually means

A card is ready when it clears four tests.

First: everyone at the refinement session can describe what done looks like in their own words without reading the ticket. If they have to check the acceptance criteria to answer, the understanding isn't there yet. The ticket is a prompt, not the understanding itself.

Second: the team knows roughly how big the work is. Rough sizing — is this a day's work or a week's work? Is it big enough to break into smaller cards, or is it appropriately scoped to pick up as-is? A card that could be anywhere from half a day to three weeks hasn't been thought through. This rough size *is* the estimate. Most of the time, that's all you need. Teams that try to convert it into something more precise — story points to two decimal places, planning poker for an hour on a single card — usually produce false confidence rather than better planning. The exception is when stakeholders need a date or a commitment. That's not a refinement problem, and a later chapter handles it directly.

Third: there are no known decision gaps that would stop the work mid-flight. Not "we can figure it out when we get there" — specifically, "we have agreed on the scope, the approach, and what the edge cases look like." The known unknowns have been converted to decisions. Unknown unknowns are unavoidable; they surface when the work starts. Known unknowns — "we haven't yet decided X" — are what refinement is supposed to eliminate.

Fourth: the card reflects the system as it actually exists today, not the system as it was when the card was written. A card written nine months ago describes a system that has changed. Before it gets picked up, someone should confirm the context is still accurate. Stale cards are decision debt wearing a refined costume. The depreciation rule from chapter 1 applies here: refinement is the value-adding process, but that value has a shelf life.

Those four tests. A card that clears them is ready. A card that doesn't, isn't — and the right move is to send it back, not to push it through.

The questions that do the work

Refinement is a conversation, and the questions that drive it matter more than the format of the output.

What does done look like? This is the single most important question in refinement. Not "what are the requirements" — too broad. Not "what should the user be able to do" — closer, but it still doesn't force enough specificity. *What does done look like* asks whoever owns the ticket to describe the completed state specifically enough that someone else can verify it. When the answer is vague — "the user should be able to complete the flow" — the card isn't ready. When the answer is specific — "the user fills in the form, hits submit, sees a confirmation screen, and receives an email within thirty seconds" — you're close.

What's the smallest version of this that delivers value? Most tickets are overspecified on the first pass. The PO has imagined the ideal version and written down everything it would include. Some of that is essential; some of it is decoration. *Smallest version* forces a conversation about what's load-bearing. The decoration becomes a follow-up card or gets dropped. This question also surfaces hidden scope — sometimes the smallest version question reveals there isn't one, that everything in the ticket is genuinely required, which is itself useful information.

Is there anything we'd need to decide that we can't decide today? This is the not-ready test. If the answer is yes — "we need to know whether the API supports X before we can scope this" — the card goes back. Not into the general backlog to age, but to whoever owns the outstanding decision, with a clear note about what's needed and by when. The refinement session doesn't wait for those decisions; it surfaces that they're missing and routes them to the right person.

What approach are we taking? Specifically for technical work. Not a full design review — just enough that the team has agreed on the general path. Two developers can hold genuinely different understandings of how a piece of work should be done, and if those understandings aren't reconciled in refinement, they get reconciled in the pull request review — at much higher cost. A brief technical discussion in refinement is cheaper than a full re-implementation after review.

The test for shared understanding

Before a card is marked ready, run the same test you run at the end of planning: ask the people who were in the room separately.

What are we building with this card?

If you get the same answer in different words, refinement worked. If you get different answers, the conversation happened but the understanding didn't form. The most common failure is a refined ticket that the PO understands and the developers don't — or vice versa, a technically clear card whose product intent is unclear. Both produce mid-flight back-and-forth that costs the same amount of time as a longer refinement session, just at the worst possible moment.

The ask-them-separately test sounds like extra work. It's actually a shortcut. Running it once per session on the card that felt haziest takes two minutes and catches the misunderstandings before they become mid-sprint blockers. Teams that skip it discover the misunderstanding on day three when the developer is halfway through and realises they've built the wrong thing.

Just-in-time, not big-batch

Refine what you need for the next sprint, plus a small buffer. Don't refine the whole backlog.

Most backlog-grooming sessions break this rule. Two hours every fortnight, a long list of tickets, everyone working through them at shallow depth. Three weeks later most of the refined cards have been deprioritised or are stale because the system moved on. The refinement investment depreciated before it was used.

I worked with a team where the opposite seemed true. The product manager and business analyst had lined up months of work, the backlog was spotless, every card had acceptance criteria in perfect gherkin format. Everyone thought it was great. Then the business analyst went on holiday for a sprint or two, and an old bug surfaced at planning. Because planning had become a rubber-stamp exercise — everything was pre-refined, so the team had no questions — the card went straight in. When someone picked it up, it didn't make sense anymore. The system had moved on so far that the bug had actually been fixed somewhere else. Nobody could recreate the issue. The acceptance criteria were so long and perfectly formatted that nobody could tell whether the card was done or not. Management asked if the high-priority bug was fixed. The team couldn't answer without support contacting the customer again. The rework required to establish that no further work was needed was significant, and the loss of confidence at senior level was real. The backlog looked refined; the understanding had evaporated.

Just-in-time refinement inverts this. You refine for depth, not breadth. The cards genuinely imminent — likely to be pulled in the next sprint or two — get real attention. The middle of the backlog stays lightly understood: the team knows roughly what those cards are, roughly how big, but the detailed conversation hasn't happened yet. Everything else is untouched. Trying to refine cards months from being picked up produces work that depreciates before it's useful.

The front of the backlog should look like a refined queue. The rest should look like a prioritised list of things the team understands well enough to estimate but hasn't decided yet. The backlog has never been and shouldn't try to be a complete specification of all future work.

This also means refinement sessions should be short. An hour, once or twice a week, covering five to eight cards at real depth. If a session consistently runs two hours or more, either the cards aren't ready to refine — they need decisions upstream that haven't been made — or the scope of the cards is too large and they need to be broken down first. Long refinement sessions are often a symptom of exactly the problem they're supposed to solve.

When a card can't be refined

Some cards arrive at refinement and can't be refined, because a decision hasn't been made upstream.

The scope is unclear because the PO hasn't decided what they want. The design hasn't been signed off. An upstream card this depends on hasn't finished. The acceptance criteria would require a technical decision that nobody has the authority or information to make today. These aren't refinement problems. They're pre-refinement problems.

Trying to refine a card without enough information just produces a clearer description of an unclear piece of work, which helps no one. The right move is to send the card back — not to the general backlog to age again, but to whoever owns the outstanding decision, with a note about what's needed before the card can be refined. The decision-owner gets a deadline: before the next refinement session, or before planning, whichever is sooner.

This is the refinement version of the standup's no-scheduled-finish-no-pull rule. Work doesn't enter refinement until the decisions upstream of it have been made. If the card can't be refined because a stakeholder hasn't made a call, the call needs to be made before the card comes back to the table.

A team that consistently has cards arrive at refinement unready has an upstream problem, not a refinement problem. The question to ask is: where in the process are decisions being deferred that should be made earlier? Usually it's the PO not engaging with the backlog between sprints, or stakeholder input arriving too late, or scope not being locked before refinement. The fix is upstream. Adding more time to the refinement session doesn't help if the inputs aren't ready.

Failure modes

Three patterns to watch for. Each one tells you something specific about what's broken.

The team refines the same cards repeatedly. A card comes up in refinement, the session goes nowhere, the card goes back to the backlog. Next fortnight, same card. Same conversation. Same result. This is the symptom of an upstream decision that hasn't been made — the card genuinely can't be refined because something is blocking it. The fix isn't to try harder in the session. It's to identify the blocking decision, name it explicitly, and route it to whoever can make it. A card that has been through refinement twice without progressing is a deferred decision with a ticket attached. Name it as such and push it to resolution.

Refinement produces tickets that can't be built. The session runs, the ticket looks refined, and then the developer picks it up and needs three conversations with the PO before work can start. This is the shared-understanding failure. The conversation happened but the understanding didn't form. The fix is to run the ask-them-separately test before cards are marked ready — particularly for any card where the refinement session felt smooth rather than substantive. Cards that go through refinement without friction often haven't actually been understood; they've been accepted.

Refinement becomes a rubber-stamp ceremony. The PO writes everything in advance. The team nods. Cards get marked ready. Nobody builds shared understanding because everything has been pre-decided and the session is a presentation rather than a conversation. This produces the same pattern as goal-handing-down in planning — the team executes without owning. The fix is to run refinement as a conversation, not a briefing. The PO brings the intent; the team helps shape the scope, the approach, and what done looks like. If the whole ticket is written before refinement, it's being written by the wrong person at the wrong time.

The rescue, in week one

Most teams you'll inherit run refinement as backlog grooming — covering many cards at low depth, often at too-long intervals. The conversion to just-in-time, shared-understanding refinement is straightforward but requires the PO to shift how they prepare.

In your first refinement session: don't work through a list. Pick three cards that are genuinely likely to be in the next sprint. Take your time with each. Ask the four questions. Go until everyone at the table can describe the card without reading it. Then stop. Three cards refined to real shared understanding is worth more than fifteen cards given a once-over.

The PO will feel this is too slow. The answer is that it isn't — it's the right speed for the job. A card that takes twenty minutes to refine properly takes twenty minutes in refinement and near zero time in mid-flight clarification. A card that takes three minutes to nominally "refine" takes three minutes in refinement and two hours of mid-sprint back-and-forth when the developer picks it up. The time doesn't disappear; it moves.

If a card can't be refined in the session because a decision is missing, don't spend time on it. Name the missing decision, assign it to whoever can make it, set a deadline, move on. Add it to next session's list once the decision has been made.

After two or three sessions, something shifts. The team starts catching unready cards before you have to. *I don't think we've actually decided what happens in the error state here.* That's the team doing its own quality control on the refinement output. When that starts happening, the rescue has taken.

The next chapter is about the retro — the ceremony where the team looks at itself. Refinement makes the next sprint's work ready to build. The retro makes the team itself better at building it.

Chapter 8: The Retro

A retro is where the team improves how it works.

Every other ceremony in this part of the book operates on the work itself. The standup moves today's cards along. Planning turns a goal into an execution plan. Refinement makes the next batch of work ready to build. The retro is the only one whose subject isn't the work — it's the team. How the team operates, where it's losing time, what it should change about the way it works. The retro is the team's process-improvement engine, and for most teams it's the only scheduled slot that job gets.

That practice — regular, deliberate improvement, made of small changes rather than occasional big ones — is what the Toyota Production System named kaizen. The premise is that a team improving one thing every couple of weeks, sustained across a year, ends up somewhere a team waiting for a single big transformation never reaches. The retro is where a software team does this. One improvement per cycle. Compounding.

Complaints are part of how it works, but they aren't the point. A problem often surfaces first as a complaint — the build is too slow, refinement runs long, nobody can find anything in the backlog. That's useful: naming what isn't working is where improvement starts, and the retro is one of the few places that naming is supposed to happen. But a complaint is raw material. The product is the improvement the team makes in response. A retro that collects complaints and produces no improvement has kept the input and thrown away the point.

If the retro isn't producing improvement — an actual, visible change in how the team works — the instrument isn't reading.

I once attended a retro where the format was: each person drew a smiley face showing how they felt that week, held it up to the group, and explained it. One person said it had been a great week because someone had brought in a birthday cake. The next person took ten minutes on their week. By the time everyone had taken a turn, the hour was gone. The team felt heard. Nothing about how the team worked had changed. The next sprint started with the same problems as the last.

From complaint to commitment

Most retros are gripe sessions. The team identifies five or ten things that aren't working, they get written on stickies, the team agrees they're problems, the meeting ends, and nothing happens. Two weeks later the same five or ten complaints come up again. Two weeks after that. Six months later the team is having the same conversation about the same problems, and nobody believes the retro can actually change anything.

This isn't a failure of the team. It's a failure of the format. Most retros are run with a structure that explicitly produces complaints — *what went well, what didn't go well, what should we do differently.* The middle column attracts everything frustrating about the sprint and turns into a list. The third column produces vague items like "communicate better" or "improve estimates," which the team agrees with but nobody owns. The action items, if any, are aspirations, not commitments.

The fix is to change what the retro produces. The output of a working retro isn't a list of complaints; it's a decision. Specifically: what is the one thing the team is going to change in the next sprint, and who is going to make sure it happens. If you can't answer those two questions when the retro ends, the retro hasn't done its job.

This sounds like an aggressive simplification, and it is. Most teams have more than one thing they want to change. Most retros surface multiple legitimate issues. The discipline of picking one isn't because there's only one issue worth addressing — it's because picking more than one means picking none.

The improvement lens

The retro works best when finding improvements isn't only the manager's job. A team where every member is looking for things to improve surfaces far more than a team where the manager brings a list and everyone else reacts to it.

What gets in the way is that most people bring an emotional lens to their work. *I liked that piece of work. I hated that one. That sprint went badly. I'm good at this part and hopeless at that one.* The emotional lens turns every piece of work into a verdict — on the sprint, on the team, on the person doing it. A verdict is a poor starting point for improvement: if hard work feels like a personal failing, the rational response is to hide it, defend it, or quietly endure it. None of those surface a kaizen.

The reframe is to trade the emotional lens for a process one. Instead of *did I like this* or *was this good*, the question becomes: *is this process under control or not?* Work that flowed smoothly is a process under control. Work that was slow, painful, error-prone, full of waiting and rework is a process not yet under control —

which is the same thing as an improvement waiting to be picked up. The deployment everyone dreads stops being a complaint, or an admission of weakness, and becomes a located problem: here is a process that isn't under control, here is a kaizen.

This is a coaching job, done one sentence at a time. When someone frames something as a like or a dislike, a good or a bad, convert it in front of them. Not *you're slow at deployments* but *the deployment process isn't under control yet — let's put it on the matrix.* Not *that was a bad sprint* but *which part of the sprint wasn't under control?* Said often enough, the team starts doing the conversion itself, and the retro fills with located problems instead of vague feelings. The impact-by-effort matrix in the next section is partly a tool for forcing this conversion — it won't accept *I hate this*; it makes you give the problem a size and a cost.

There's a quieter benefit. When a hard piece of work is a process problem rather than a personal one, it stops carrying shame — which is easier on the person and also more accurate, because most painful work is the product of an underbuilt process, not a deficient person.

Causes, not labels

It's worth saying at the start of every retro that the team is examining two things, not one: what went well, and what went badly. Most retros only do the second. That's half a retro.

Both halves are the same activity — root cause analysis. When something went badly, the team finds what caused it and changes it. When something went well, the team finds what caused it and does more of it. The piece of work that sailed through, the release that didn't generate a single support ticket, the refinement session that left everyone clear — none of that was luck. Something produced it, and if the team can name what, it can make it repeatable. A team that only ever analyses its failures improves at half the rate of a team that also analyses its successes, because it's discarding every lesson that arrives wearing good news.

The emotional label — *that went well, that was painful* — is only the starting point. The value is one question further in: *why?* A retro that stops at the label has collected feelings. A retro that goes to the cause has found something it can act on, in either direction. This is the same move as the improvement lens: don't stop at the verdict, find the process underneath it.

The impact-by-effort matrix

Chapter 1 introduced the impact-by-effort matrix as the diagnostic tool the team uses in its first retro to surface what's worth acting on. The same matrix is the format every subsequent retro should use, because it does two things at once. It surfaces items and ranks them. The output isn't a list of issues — it's an issue with a position on a 2x2 grid that tells the team where to spend its attention.

Briefly: each item the team raises gets placed on the matrix according to two axes. How much impact would fixing it have on the team's work? How much effort would the fix require? The top-left quadrant — high impact, low effort — is where the team should always look first. The top-right quadrant — high impact, high effort — is where strategic conversations belong, but most weeks the team shouldn't be picking from there. The bottom half is mostly noise, and the discipline of putting things there explicitly is what stops them from absorbing the team's attention.

The matrix has a side-effect that makes retros run better: it forces the team to think about effort, not just impact. Teams that don't use it end up identifying problems by importance and then committing to actions that nobody can actually do. The matrix surfaces the gap between "this matters" and "this is fixable." A high-impact, high-effort item often ends up being something the team can't actually fix in a sprint — and naming that explicitly, putting it in the top-right and acknowledging it's a strategic conversation rather than a tactical one, frees the team to focus on what they can do.

The matrix is filled in collaboratively. Five to ten minutes of silent writing on stickies; five minutes of placing them on the grid; ten minutes of clustering and discussing. By the end of twenty-five minutes, the team has a ranked picture of what's worth acting on, with a top-left quadrant that contains the candidates for the sprint's one action.

The timeline exercise

The matrix surveys a whole sprint at once. Sometimes the more useful move is to go deep on a single piece of work, and the timeline exercise is how you do it.

Take one piece of work — a feature that just shipped, an incident, a release, something that went unusually badly or unusually well — and draw its timeline on a whiteboard. Then mark everything that happened along it: the decisions, the handoffs, the waits, the moments it stalled, the moments it moved fast, the points where someone had to go back and redo something. The team builds the timeline together, because no one person saw all of it.

Then walk the timeline from start to finish and stop at each point with one question: with hindsight, is there something we'd do differently here? Sometimes the answer is a problem — a three-day wait for a review nobody chased, a decision that should have been made a week earlier. Sometimes it's the opposite — a point where something went right, and the team can see what produced it. Either way, the team has found a candidate improvement located at a specific point in a real sequence, rather than floating as a general impression.

This is root cause analysis with the timeline doing the work of jogging memory. It surfaces things a sprint-level survey misses, because people remember a sequence of concrete events far more accurately than they remember a general feeling about the last two weeks. It isn't an every-retro exercise — the matrix is the regular cadence. The timeline is for when a particular piece of work is worth the depth, or when the matrix keeps surfacing the same vague issue and the team needs to see it laid out concretely. As with the matrix, it will surface several candidate improvements; the team still picks one.

Here is one that came out of a timeline retro. We were building an API against a specification document from a third-party vendor whose system ours had to talk to. From the start, I tried to get the vendor to test our work as we finished each iteration. They had no time. I wrote to the client manager, then to their higher-ups, then asked our own management to lean on theirs. Still no time. So we built in the dark — we wrote our own test data from the spec, pumped it through the API, and watched it pass. By the spec, the thing worked.

Then the vendor scheduled the integration for a single week, finally ran our API against their real system, and it fell over, exactly as we had been warning for months.

In the retro we drew the timeline of the whole build and walked it. The team's first instinct was to find the point where we should have escalated harder, or sooner, or to someone different. But every time someone placed an improvement at one of those points, someone else said *we did that* — and we had. The escalation was never the miss.

The miss was at the very start of the timeline, before a line of code. We should have hand-crafted a small text file of expected inputs and outputs straight from the spec and asked the vendor to validate just that — not to test a system, just to read a page. A vendor with no time to test an integration can nearly always find twenty minutes to check a file. If our reading of the spec was wrong, that file would have exposed it in the first week, for almost nothing, instead of in the last week, for the price of the entire build.

The point isn't the file. It's that the improvement worth having was nowhere near the part of the story the team wanted to talk about — and only walking the timeline all the way back to its beginning surfaced it.

One thing

The team picks one thing and commits to it — one item from the matrix's top-left quadrant, or one improvement from the timeline.

Not three. Not "the top three." One. The discipline is to commit fully to a single action because the team has finite attention, and an action that has 100% of the team's attention is more likely to ship than three actions that have 33% each. The math isn't quite that clean — but the principle is. Pick one. Do it. Move on to the next thing in the next retro.

The team's natural inclination is to resist this. Multiple things feel pickable. Each individual action seems small enough to do. The case for "let's do all five" feels stronger than the case for "let's pick one." The case for "let's pick one" is exactly the case the manager has to make, and it's worth making explicitly: *we've tried picking five before. It didn't work. We pick one because picking one is the only thing that's ever worked.*

The action needs an owner. Not "the team" — a person. Someone whose job between this retro and the next is to make sure the change happens. If nobody volunteers, the manager has to assign someone, because an action without an owner is a wish.

The action also needs a definition of done. Not aspirational — specific. *We will reduce the number of cards in the blocked column from twelve to four by the next retro* is a definition of done. *We will improve our handling of blocked work* is not. The definition lets the next retro answer the question of whether the change happened.

Holding the action accountable

The next retro starts with one question: *did we do the thing we committed to last time?*

If yes, what happened? Did it work? Should we keep going? Was the impact what we expected, or did it surface something else? If no, why not? What got in the way? Was the action the wrong thing, or the right thing badly executed, or the right thing the team couldn't get to?

This sequence sounds bureaucratic. It isn't. It's the only thing that makes retros work over time. A retro that doesn't follow up on its previous commitment teaches the team that commitments don't matter. A retro that does follow up, even briefly, teaches the team that the commitments are real.

The pattern to watch for is the team that consistently fails to do the thing they committed to. Not occasionally — consistently. If three retros in a row have failed to ship the action, the problem isn't the actions. It's the commitment process. Either the team is committing to things it doesn't actually intend to do, or there's something between commitment and execution that's breaking it. Both diagnoses are worth the next retro's attention. Either is more important than picking yet another action that won't happen.

In a healthy retro cadence, the previous-action review takes five to ten minutes. In a stuck retro cadence, it takes the whole meeting — and that's the right meeting to have, because until the team can actually execute on what it commits to, picking new commitments is theatre.

What doesn't belong in retro

A retro is a sprint-cadence ceremony. Things that shouldn't wait two weeks shouldn't be saved for the retro.

Urgent issues get raised now. The team channel, a direct conversation, a quick standup topic — whatever surfaces the issue and gets it acted on. The retro is for patterns, not for emergencies. If something urgent is held back for the retro, it's been allowed to fester for two weeks, which is two weeks the team didn't have to lose.

Personal conflicts between two team members don't belong in the retro. They get handled privately, not in front of the whole team. A retro that becomes a forum for one person to raise a grievance against another has become something else, and the manager should redirect it. The conversation matters; the venue is wrong.

Issues above the team's pay grade — leadership decisions, organisational structure, strategic direction — don't get fixed in the retro, but they can be named and escalated from it. The retro is where the team decides *we're going to escalate this to X*, with someone owning the escalation. Discussing the issue endlessly without ever escalating produces the same nine-months-of-the-same-complaint pattern that makes retros feel pointless.

The retro is for the patterns the team can address itself. Process changes, ceremony tweaks, working agreements, technical debt the team can prioritise, communication patterns within the team. The set of things that the team has agency over and that affect how the team works.

When the same things keep coming up

If a retro keeps surfacing the same issue and the team keeps not addressing it, one of three things is true.

The team can't address it — it's above their pay grade, and the retro should produce an escalation rather than a solution attempt. *We've raised this in three retros. We can't fix it ourselves. We're going to escalate to [person]. [Owner] will do it before the next retro.* That makes the issue someone else's problem in a structured way, which is the team's actual leverage.

The team won't address it — the issue is fixable but nobody actually wants to fix it because the workaround has become comfortable. The blocked column nobody talks to. The recurring meeting nobody can defend. The over-engineered process that's protecting somebody's territory. The fix here isn't to keep raising it; it's to ask the team directly *do we actually want to change this?* If the answer is no, the issue stops belonging in the retro. If the answer is yes, then the previous-action review will hold them accountable.

The issue isn't actually a problem — it's a feeling. *Communication could be better* often falls into this category. The team isn't pointing at a specific failure of communication; they're expressing a vague discomfort. Vague discomforts don't have actions. The retro can name the feeling and ask the team to surface it more specifically next sprint, but it shouldn't try to manufacture an action for a problem that hasn't been articulated. A poorly defined problem produces a poorly defined action.

The diagnostic question the manager asks when the same thing keeps coming up: *what would actually have to change for this issue to stop being on the list?* The answer reveals which of the three patterns is in play.

Cadence and format

End of every sprint. Sixty minutes. The team plus anyone whose decisions the retro depends on — usually that's just the team, but occasionally the PO if the issue concerns product decisions, or a stakeholder if the team is escalating up.

The agenda is simple. Five to ten minutes on the previous retro's action — did we do it, what happened. Twenty-five minutes on the impact-by-effort matrix — silent writing, placement, clustering, discussion. Twenty minutes on the new action — pick one, decide what done looks like, assign an owner, set the deadline, which is the next retro. Five to ten minutes of buffer for any escalation conversations or working agreement updates.

The first retro after you join a team — chapter 1 covers this — is longer, ninety minutes, because it's covering the whole observation period rather than a single sprint. After that, sixty minutes is the right shape. Going longer regularly is a sign that the retro is doing too many jobs. Going shorter is a sign that the team has stopped engaging with it.

Failure modes

Three patterns to watch for after the rescue. Each tells you something specific.

The retro produced an action but nobody did it. Next retro discovers nothing has changed. The action's owner says they got busy. Someone suggests picking a smaller action next time. This is the single most common retro failure, and the fix is uncomfortable: refuse to pick a new action until the previous one is shipped or explicitly abandoned. The team is committing to things it doesn't actually intend to do, and the manager has to interrupt that pattern before it becomes "we never do anything we commit to."

The retro picks five things, does none of them. Variant of the above, more aggressive. The team feels accomplished after the meeting because it identified many issues. Two weeks later, none of the issues have been addressed, but new issues have appeared. The fix is to enforce one. *We pick one because we have a pattern of picking five and doing none. Until we can ship one consistently, we don't get to pick more.* The team will resist this, because picking one feels like under-committing. The team is wrong. Picking five and doing none is what under-committing actually looks like.

The retro produces escalations that never happen. *We need to raise this with leadership* is the action. Two weeks later, leadership hasn't been raised with. Pattern repeats. The retro has become a place where issues go to die — they get acknowledged, they get nominally escalated, and the escalation never happens because the team's owner of it didn't actually do it or didn't know how. The fix is the same as the action-not-shipped pattern: hold the escalation accountable. *We said you'd raise this with [person] by [date]. Did you? If not, what got in the way?* If the team's escalation owner can't actually do the escalation, the manager needs to find someone who can, including possibly themselves.

The rescue, in week one

Most retros you'll inherit produce complaints, not change. The conversion is straightforward but the team has to feel it before they trust it.

Your first retro: don't run the format the team is used to. Run the impact-by-effort matrix. Explain why before you start: *we're going to identify problems and rank them by impact and effort, and we're going to pick one to commit to as a team. One, not five.* The team will be sceptical. The scepticism is fine. Run the matrix anyway.

Pick the top-left item — high impact, low effort — and ask the team if anyone wants to own the change. If someone volunteers, they own it. If nobody volunteers, you have to make it specific enough that volunteering is easy: *the action is to delete the recurring sync that nobody can defend. Who's going to send the calendar invite cancellation? It takes thirty seconds.* Reluctance to volunteer for a change that takes thirty seconds is a useful diagnostic — usually it means the change has more political weight than it looks like. Name that, and decide whether to push through or pick something else.

Set the deadline as the next retro, two weeks out. Start the next retro by asking whether it happened. If yes, celebrate briefly and move on. If no, the conversation is *why didn't it happen, and what does the team need to do differently next time?*

Within three or four sprints, the team should be shipping the retro action they committed to. That's the indicator that the rescue has taken. If after six retros the team is still failing to ship its committed action, you have a deeper problem — usually trust or accountability, and chapter 3 is the relevant lens.

The next chapter is about the demo — the team's feedback loop with the people outside it, where the work finally meets the judgement of whoever it's for. The retro turned the team's experience into a decision about how it works; the demo turns the work itself into a decision about whether it's heading the right way.

Chapter 9: The Demo

A demo is not a show-and-tell. It is the moment a stakeholder with skin in the game looks at the actual work and decides whether it is heading the right way — while there is still time to change course. A demo that produces no such decision is theatre.

That is the whole test, and most demos fail it. The team gathers, the work gets shown, the stakeholders nod, everyone says "great progress," and nothing is decided. The meeting felt productive. It produced a feeling, not a decision. Two sprints later the same work gets shown again, a little further along, and again nothing is decided, until eventually it ships and someone says "this isn't quite what I expected" — at the one moment when changing course is most expensive.

The demo exists to stop exactly that. It is a feedback loop like every other one in this part: information goes in — here is what we built — and a decision comes out — keep going, change this, stop that. If no decision comes out, the loop is broken, and you are holding a meeting with the right name and the wrong job.

The two schools

Before you can run a demo well, you have to know which kind of demo the person watching it thinks they are attending. There are two, and they are genuinely different.

The first is the agile-leaning view: a demo shows what the team managed to produce in the time it had. The work is an increment. It may be rough, partial, unpolished — the point is to show real progress early enough that the direction can still be corrected cheaply. The demo is a checkpoint, and "this is not finished" is an expected and acceptable thing to say in the room.

The second is the milestone view, common among people who run projects on Gantt charts: a demo shows a finished, working product that has reached a defined milestone. The work is meant to be done. "This is not finished" is not an acceptable thing to say — it reads as failure to hit the milestone. The demo is a gate, not a checkpoint.

Both are legitimate. Different stakeholders, different industries, different temperaments land in different camps, and neither is wrong on its own terms. What is always wrong is mismatching them. If you give a milestone-minded stakeholder an agile increment — rough, half-built, shown early for feedback — they will not see a useful checkpoint. They will see an unfinished product presented as if it were done, and they will react accordingly. If you give an agile-minded stakeholder a polished milestone demo where the only thing left to decide is the colours and the fonts, you have wasted everyone's time, because there was no real decision left to make by the time they saw it. The whole value — course-correction — was already gone.

So the first move with any demo is not preparing the software. It is working out what the person watching expects to see, and making sure what you bring matches it. Get that wrong and the demo produces confrontation instead of a decision, no matter how good the work is.

A demo produces a decision, or it is theatre

The clearest signal that a demo is doing its job is that real questions get asked and a direction decision comes out the other side. The clearest signal that it is theatre is a parade of features met with polite nods.

I worked with a product owner once who was genuinely engaged — she came to every demo, and she brought the actual person who used the software. Near the end of the project, with the thing being wound down, we had two weeks left to build the last few features at the top of the backlog. One of the developers had an idea: a keyboard shortcut for a particular function. It seemed obvious to the engineers — who wouldn't want a shortcut that saved all those clicks? At a demo we raised it as the next thing to build.

The product owner and the user looked confused. Why would anyone need that? They used that function maybe once a quarter, and on the rare occasion they did, clicking it with the mouse was just as fast — it only ever changed one record at a time. The shortcut would have saved nobody anything. That demo, and the two questions asked in it, saved about three days of development out of the two weeks we had left. And it surfaced what actually mattered: a bulk-edit function for something else entirely, sitting ten rows down the backlog, turned out to be the most pressing thing we could build. We built that instead.

That is a demo working. Not because the software impressed anyone, but because the people with skin in the game asked real questions and a direction decision came out — don't build the shortcut, build the bulk edit. Three days of waste avoided and the most valuable remaining feature identified, in one conversation, because the right people were in the room and the demo was a place where decisions were allowed to happen.

The waste the keyboard shortcut would have been is the kind that is invisible without the demo. The developers were not being foolish — the feature was locally sensible, it just served nobody. Left to its own logic, engineering builds the thing that is satisfying to build. The demo is where someone who actually uses the software gets to say "I would never use that," before the three days are spent rather than after.

Set the expectation before the demo, not during it

The most expensive demo I ever ran taught me that telling a stakeholder what to expect is not the same as making sure they expect it.

I was working with a team whose senior stakeholder had decided everything would be built in a low-code platform using only its standard modules. The team kept hitting cases the standard modules couldn't handle and arguing they needed custom components. The senior stakeholder kept insisting it could be done in modules. This had gridlocked the work for months: the team would build something custom, and at release it would get questioned and pushed back. To make it worse, only the senior stakeholder had the domain expertise to validate whether the work actually met the requirements — it was an industry without much of a software culture — so there was no independent way to settle the argument. He had come to deeply distrust the team, and the distrust fed the gridlock.

A shelved project came up that he suddenly wanted started immediately, with requirements nobody was confident were properly understood. In all my wisdom, I decided the way to break the impasse was a demo. I'd get the team to build the first week's work — a small increment, rough, early enough that we could course-correct hard if the requirements were wrong, and concrete enough to finally test whether modules or custom components were the answer. I would settle both arguments at once. I briefed the senior stakeholder carefully. I told him, several times, that this would be a very rough first draft and the entire point was to course-correct early.

The team worked themselves into the ground to get something running. The day came. They showed him what they'd built. He launched into a shouting tirade about what a piece of shit it was and how it didn't do anything.

He had missed the point of the session entirely — and I had missed his expectation of what a demo was, despite telling him repeatedly what to expect. He was a milestone man. To him a demo meant a finished thing that worked. No amount of me saying "this is a rough draft for course-correction" had moved him off that, because I had stated the expectation without ever confirming he'd actually accepted it. I told. I didn't check that it landed. And the deeper failure underneath it was the same one that had gridlocked the whole engagement: the relationship ran on telling, not asking. He told the team it could be done in modules; they told him it couldn't; I told him what a demo was. Nobody, including me, was asking.

The lesson generalises past that one furious afternoon. Stating the expected format of a demo is necessary and not sufficient. You have to confirm the stakeholder is actually in the same school you are — and if you can't get them there, you give the demo they expect, not the one you wish they wanted. With a milestone-minded stakeholder who cannot be moved, you do not show rough early increments. You wait until you have something that meets their definition of working, or you find a different mechanism than a demo to get your course-correction. Forcing an agile demo on a milestone stakeholder doesn't convert them. It just detonates.

Who needs to be in the room

A demo only produces a decision if the person who can make the decision is watching it.

This sounds obvious and is constantly violated. The demo gets shown to a proxy — a delegate, a junior stakeholder, someone "representing" the decision-maker — and real questions get deferred because the person in the room can't actually answer them. The result is a demo that looks like the others, produces the usual nods, and decides nothing, because the only person who could decide wasn't there. Then the real decision-maker sees it late, in a different setting, with none of the context, and reacts to the finished thing — which is the most expensive possible moment for them to first engage.

The rule is the same as the one in the planning chapter: whoever's decision the work depends on needs to be in the room when the work is shown. For most product work that is whoever owns the direction — the product owner, the sponsoring stakeholder, the person who will live with the result. Where possible, also the person who actually uses the software, because they are the ones who will tell you the keyboard shortcut is useless before you build it. A demo to people who can only spectate is a demo that cannot do its job.

Failure modes

Demos fail in recognisable ways. Most of them are the same failure — no decision — wearing different clothes.

The parade of features. The team walks through everything it built, screen by screen, and the stakeholders nod along. There are no real questions because nothing is being asked of them — they are an audience, not a decision-making body. The fix is to stop presenting and start asking: *here's what we built; is this the right direction, and what should we do next?* Put a decision on the table and refuse to end the meeting until one is made.

The decision-maker isn't in the room. The demo runs for proxies who can't commit, so nothing gets decided and the real reaction arrives late and expensive. The fix is upstream — don't run the demo until the person whose decision the work depends on can attend, even if that means moving it.

The over-rehearsed demo. The team has practised the demo so thoroughly, on such a controlled happy path, that it no longer surfaces anything real. Every input is the input that works; every click is the click that's been tested. It looks flawless and tells you nothing, because the point of a demo is to find the problems while they're cheap, and a demo engineered to hide problems has inverted its own purpose. The fix is to demo the real thing, rough edges included, and to actively go looking for the cases that break it in the room.

The endless demo — the fail loop. Every demo produces a fresh round of "you've missed this" and "what about this edge case," the work never converges, and the project loops indefinitely without ever shipping. Sometimes this is genuine discovery. But when it goes on too long, when every demo finds a new gap no matter how many you close, the root cause is usually not in the demo at all. It is upstream, in the stakeholder relationship — someone who, for reasons that have nothing to do with the software, does not actually want it to ship. No demo technique fixes that, because the demo is not where the problem lives. That one belongs to the stakeholder chapter, and it is where we'll pick it up.

The rescue, in week one

If you inherit a team whose demos are theatre, the conversion is direct.

Before the next demo, find out which school each key stakeholder is in. Ask them, plainly, what they expect to see — a work-in-progress checkpoint, or a finished milestone. Don't assume; the senior stakeholder taught me that. Then bring the demo that matches what they told you, and confirm the match out loud at the start of the session: *this is an early increment, rough on purpose, and what I want from you today is a decision about direction.* Naming the contract at the top means nobody is sitting there expecting a finished product while you show them scaffolding.

Make sure the person who can actually decide is in the room, and the person who actually uses the software too, if you can get them. Then, at the demo, put a real decision on the table and don't let the meeting end until it's made. *Is this the right direction? What's the most valuable next thing? Is there anything here we should stop?* The first time a demo kills a feature that wasn't worth building, or surfaces the thing ten rows down the backlog that turns out to matter most, the team will feel the difference between a demo and a status parade.

The signal the rescue has taken is simple: demos start ending with decisions, and the team stops being ambushed — by a furious stakeholder, by a late change of direction, by three days spent building a shortcut nobody wanted. Information in, decision out, work moves. Same test as every loop in this part.

The demo is the team's feedback loop with the people outside it — the place where the team's work meets the judgement of whoever it's for. The retro, earlier in this part, was the loop the team runs on itself; the demo is the loop it runs with the outside world. The next chapter turns to estimation — what happens when those outside stakeholders want a date, and the team doesn't have one.

Chapter 10: Estimation, Commitments, and the Date Question

ESTIMATION, in most teams, isn't really about measurement. It's about answering the question *when?*

The team is asked when something will be done. The team gives a number. The number is wrong. Everyone knows the number is likely to be wrong, but everyone pretends otherwise, because the alternative — saying *I don't know* — has become culturally unacceptable in most companies. So the wrong number gets recorded. Plans get built on it. And when the work doesn't ship by the date, the stakeholder feels deceived and the team feels punished.

This chapter isn't about how to estimate. The shelves are full of books about how to estimate, and they're full because none of the techniques fundamentally work — none of them can convert work whose nature isn't fully understood into a precise time prediction. They give the appearance of precision without the substance. The chapter is about what to do when stakeholders need a date and the team genuinely doesn't have one.

The reframing: estimation is mostly a communication problem, not a measurement problem. The teams that handle dates well aren't better at predicting the future. They're better at telling stakeholders the truth about what they know and don't know, in a form the stakeholder can actually plan around.

What rough sizing already gives you

Chapter 7 made the case that refinement produces a rough size as one of its outputs, and most of the time that rough size is the estimate. *This is a day's work. This is a week's work. This is too big to scope, break it down.* That's enough for the team to plan a sprint. It's enough for the team to know whether a card fits in the next two weeks or doesn't. It's enough for almost every internal planning conversation.

What rough sizing doesn't give you is a date. *A week's work* doesn't tell the stakeholder when the work will be done, because it doesn't say which week, and because the team will be doing other work alongside it, and because the upstream dependency might slip, and because the integration with another team might surface an issue that adds three days. None of those are estimation problems. They're scheduling problems, dependency problems, capacity problems. Trying to solve them by making the size estimate more precise is solving the wrong problem.

The first move when a stakeholder asks *when will this be done* is to clarify what they're actually asking. Most stakeholders aren't asking for a point estimate. They're asking because they have something they need to coordinate — a marketing launch, a board update, a customer commitment, another team's work that depends on yours. The thing they actually need is enough information to plan around. Sometimes that's a date with a confidence range. Sometimes it's a milestone. Sometimes it's just a heads-up that the work is or isn't on the critical path. Knowing what the stakeholder actually needs prevents the team from over-committing to precision the situation doesn't require.

Forecasts, not estimates

When the stakeholder genuinely needs a date, give them a forecast, not an estimate.

The distinction matters. An estimate is a point prediction: *this will take three weeks.* A forecast is a range with explicit assumptions: *based on the team's recent delivery rate, and assuming the platform team ships their API change by next Wednesday, this completes between weeks four and seven.*

Three differences land between those two answers. The forecast is honest about uncertainty rather than concealing it. The forecast names the assumptions, which lets the stakeholder push back on them or work around them. And the forecast gives a range, which is what stakeholders actually need to plan — they want to know the latest the work could realistically arrive, not the date the team thinks is most likely.

Stakeholders sometimes resist forecasts because the range feels evasive. *Just give me a date.* The honest response is that a date is a forecast with the range hidden — it's the same uncertainty, with the team having absorbed all the risk of being wrong. The team that gives a date is the team that gets blamed when the date slips. The team that gives a forecast with explicit assumptions is the team that can point at the assumption that broke when the work slipped, which is the actual cause.

If a stakeholder forces a single date, the move is to give the late end of the range. *We forecast this between week four and week seven, so let's plan around week seven.* That isn't sandbagging — it's the honest answer to *when is the latest this could realistically be done.* If the work ships in week four, everyone celebrates. If it ships in week seven, the plan held. The downside is asymmetric, and giving the early end of the range is what produces most of the trust damage in stakeholder relationships.

Velocity-based forecasting

When the team has been together for a while and has a track record, the cleanest forecasting method is the simplest one: look at how much work the team has actually been completing per sprint, and use that.

If the team has finished an average of 30 points of work over the last six sprints, with a range of 24 to 35, then a 90-point body of work is forecast at *between three and four sprints*. That's it. No story-point math. No formula. Just the team's actual delivery rate applied to the actual work.

This is more honest than estimation-from-first-principles for two reasons. It integrates everything the team has been dealing with — the meetings, the support tickets, the reviews, the rework — rather than treating those as friction to be subtracted from a theoretical capacity. And it's based on what the team has actually shipped, not what the team thinks it ought to be able to ship if everything went well.

Velocity-based forecasting requires consistency in how work is sized. The team doesn't need to estimate brilliantly; it needs to estimate the same way over time. A team that estimates with t-shirt sizes will get a useful forecast just by counting cards-of-each-size completed per sprint. A team that estimates with story points will get a forecast as long as the points mean roughly the same thing this sprint as they did last sprint. The technique matters less than the consistency.

When the team has a real body of throughput data — ideally a couple of months of completed work per sprint — there's a more rigorous version worth using. Monte Carlo forecasting takes the team's actual sprint-by-sprint history and runs the remaining work through it thousands of times, sampling from that real distribution instead of assuming an average. The output isn't a single date or even a simple range; it's a probability. *There's an 85% chance this is done within six sprints, and a 50% chance within four.* That's about as honest as a forecast gets, because it states the uncertainty as a number instead of hiding it. It's the one estimation technique from the textbooks that earns its place in this book, for that exact reason. It needs a decent sample of throughput data to work — a brand-new team won't have it — but once a team does, it's worth the small effort to set up.

The major caveat is that the work being forecast has to be similar to the work the team has been doing. If the next quarter is a system rebuild and the past quarter was feature work, the velocity number is going to mislead. The team's forecast should explicitly note this: *based on our velocity in feature work, but the next quarter is mostly platform work, so this is a soft forecast that we'll update once we have a sprint or two of platform work as a baseline.* Naming the limitation is what prevents the forecast from being weaponised later.

What the board already knows

A team I worked with kept missing its sprint commitments, and everyone — the team included — had decided the problem was bad estimation. I didn't think it was. The estimates looked honest to me. A story sized at three days of work was, as far as I could tell, about three days of work. The team just never finished what it took on.

So in a retro I picked one story that had recently shipped — an ordinary one, nothing unusual about it — and we walked its history across the board. To do. In progress. In review. Blocked. In progress again. Review again. Done. Then I asked the team to add up the calendar days the story had spent in each column.

The work had taken three days. The story had spent nineteen days on the board.

Of those nineteen days, three were work and sixteen were waiting. Four days in review, because the one person who could review it was busy with something else. Six days in the blocked column, waiting on an answer from another team. Two days sitting in to-do after the story had been "committed" but before anyone picked it up. The rest went to a second trip through review and a handoff nobody had chased.

The estimate was never wrong. Three days was an honest number for the work. But the team had been making its commitments in work time and then living in elapsed time, and the two had almost nothing to do with each other. A sprint full of three-day stories does not fit in a sprint if each story takes nineteen days to cross the board.

This is the most useful exercise I know for a team that keeps missing what it commits to. Take a finished story, walk its columns, add up the days. The total is almost always a shock, and almost always mostly waiting. Once a team has seen its own elapsed time, the question it asks when it commits changes — from *how many days of work fit into two weeks* to *how much can our process actually move across the board in two weeks.* The second number is smaller, and it's honest. You can't commit to what your process can't handle, and until the team has added up the columns, it doesn't know what its process can handle.

It also moves the problem to where it actually is. This team had come to believe it was bad at estimating. It wasn't — it was bad at flow: other people's review queues, another team's unanswered question, work marked "committed" days before anyone could start it. None of that improves by estimating harder. And to be clear about what the exercise does and doesn't do — walking the board didn't make this team faster. The sixteen waiting days were still there the next sprint. What changed is that the team stopped committing as though the waiting didn't exist; its commitments got smaller, and it started hitting them. Speeding the work up was a separate job, most of it living in that blocked column — a problem a later part of this book takes on directly.

This is also the honest answer to why velocity, from the previous section, is more trustworthy than adding up work-time estimates. A team's velocity already contains all sixteen of those waiting days, because it counts what actually reached done, not what should have. The board walkthrough just shows the team, concretely, why its velocity is the number it is.

When the team has no track record

The hardest version of the date question comes early. A team forms. Two weeks in — before it has finished a single sprint, before there's any velocity data, before anyone knows how the team actually works together — someone asks when the work will be done. And then keeps asking.

There's no honest forecast available here, and the chapter's earlier advice doesn't rescue you: velocity-based forecasting needs velocity, walking the board needs finished stories, and a two-week-old team has neither. The temptation is to manufacture a number to make the asking stop. Don't. A number invented in week two, with no empirical basis, is the worst kind of commitment — it carries all the binding force of a real forecast and none of the grounding. It will be wrong, and it will be remembered as a promise.

What you can honestly offer is two things: a forecast explicitly labelled as having no empirical basis yet, and a date by which you will have one. *We can't forecast this credibly until we've completed two or three sprints and have a sense of the team's actual throughput — that puts a real forecast about six weeks out. Until then, anything I give you is a guess, and neither of us should plan around a guess.* Most reasonable stakeholders can work with that, because it comes with a commitment attached: a date when the uncertainty resolves.

There's a second move, and it's the one most people miss. The stakeholder hounding a new team for a delivery date is very often part of the reason the date is uncertain. The person asking *when will it be done* in week two is sometimes the same person who hasn't organised system logins for the developers, or hasn't cleared access to the test environment, or hasn't decided what the first release actually needs to contain. The forecast has assumptions, and some of those assumptions are things the person asking for the forecast controls. Naming that isn't a deflection — it's the most useful thing you can do for them. *I'll give you a forecast the moment two things are true: the team has a sprint or two behind it, and the developers can actually log in to the systems they're supposed to be working on. The second one is in your hands — can we get it sorted this week?* That reframes the conversation from extracting a number to clearing the path, which is the actual work.

When you genuinely don't know

Sometimes the team doesn't have enough information to forecast at all. The work is in territory the team hasn't been in before. The dependencies aren't clear. The shape of the solution isn't decided. The team isn't being lazy or political when they say they don't know — they actually don't.

The wrong response is to estimate anyway. The team that says *I don't know* and then is pressured into giving a number gives a number that's wrong, and that wrong number gets locked in. *I don't know but if you push me three weeks* becomes *the team committed to three weeks.* The pressure to estimate doesn't produce better information; it produces fake information.

The right response is to convert the unknown into a known with a spike. A spike is a time-boxed investigation — a few days, no more — whose explicit job is to make the work scopable. The next chapter is about spikes; for the purposes of this one, the move is to say to the stakeholder: *we don't have enough information to forecast this. We need three days to investigate. After that, we'll come back with a forecast that has assumptions we can defend.*

Stakeholders rarely refuse a three-day spike if it produces a real forecast at the end. What they refuse is open-ended uncertainty, which is what the team is implicitly asking them to accept when they say *we don't know.* The spike turns *we don't know* into *we'll know by Wednesday*, which is much easier for the stakeholder to plan around. The three days isn't lost; it's the price of an honest forecast.

A team that consistently can't forecast without spikes has a different problem — usually that it's working in territory too unfamiliar too often, or that its refinement isn't producing enough understanding upstream. That's a chapter 7 conversation, not a chapter 10 one.

The story-points-as-productivity trap

Story points were invented to abstract away from time. The original idea was that estimating in points instead of hours would let teams size work relatively, without committing to durations they couldn't actually predict. The points were never supposed to be a productivity metric.

In practice, in most large organisations, that's exactly what they've become. *Velocity* gets reported up. Teams get pressure to do more points per sprint. Sprint-over-sprint point trends get scrutinised. Manager performance gets evaluated against team velocity. The whole apparatus has turned into the time-based estimation it was supposed to replace, with extra abstraction that makes it slightly harder to argue with.

The book's position is that story points are fine as a refinement tool — they help the team size work consistently and forecast based on velocity. They are not a productivity metric and should not be reported to anyone outside the team in that frame. If leadership needs to track team output, the right metrics are usually outcome-based, not point-based: features shipped, customer-facing changes, goals achieved per sprint. The team that's gaming its velocity to look good is producing the same dysfunction as a team that's gaming any other metric — Goodhart's law, applied to agile.

The corrective when leadership asks for velocity reporting isn't always to refuse. Sometimes it's to redirect: *velocity is what we use internally for forecasting. Here's what we shipped this quarter against the goals we committed to. That's the right metric for what you're trying to track.* Most leadership conversations that look like they need velocity actually need outcomes. Reframing the conversation is part of the team's job.

Failure modes

Three patterns to watch for.

The team gives point estimates and gets punished for them. Stakeholder asks when. Team says three weeks. Work takes five. Stakeholder is unhappy. Next time the team adds buffer — they say six weeks. Work takes five. Stakeholder is unhappy that the team sandbagged. The team is now in a no-win position. The fix is to stop giving point estimates and start giving forecasts with ranges and assumptions. The first time the team does this, the stakeholder may push back. The second time, they'll start to understand the discipline. By the third or fourth, they'll prefer it — because the forecast that names its assumptions is more useful for planning than the point estimate that hides them.

The team estimates everything except the dependencies. Cards get sized in story points. Forecasts get built. Then the deployment slips because devops was busy, or the integration breaks because another team's work wasn't ready. The forecast misses by a week and everyone treats it as an estimation failure.

It isn't. It's a dependency failure that the estimation framing concealed. The fix is to name dependencies explicitly in every forecast: *this completes by week six, assuming devops ships X and the platform team has Y ready.* When the assumption breaks, the forecast updates, and the conversation is about the broken assumption rather than the broken estimate.

The team is forecasting work that hasn't been refined. The PO asks for a forecast on a card that hasn't been through refinement. The team gives one anyway. The forecast is wrong because the work itself isn't understood. The fix is to refuse to forecast unrefined work. *I can't give you a useful forecast on this until we've refined it. The next refinement session is Thursday. Can it wait until Friday for the forecast?* Most stakeholders will wait. The ones who won't are usually trying to lock the team into a commitment before the team understands the work, which is exactly the trap the team needs to avoid.

The rescue, in week one

Most teams you'll inherit give point estimates that don't hold and then get blamed when they don't hold. The conversion to forecasts is straightforward but requires the team to feel that you'll back them when stakeholders push back.

Your first stakeholder estimation conversation: don't give a point estimate. Give a range with assumptions. *We forecast this between weeks four and seven, assuming the platform team ships their endpoint by Wednesday and assuming we don't pick up additional support load.* Watch how the stakeholder responds. Most stakeholders will accept the range; some will push back asking for *just a date.* When that happens, give the late end of the range and explain the choice: *if we have to commit to a single date, we commit to week seven, because that's the date we can hold even if our assumptions break.*

If the stakeholder pushes for an earlier date, the team's negotiating position is the assumptions. *We could commit to week five if we have certainty on the platform team's delivery and if we're not absorbing any new support work for the duration. Can we get that?* That puts the stakeholder in the position of resolving the actual blockers rather than pressuring the team to absorb the uncertainty.

When work eventually does or doesn't hit the forecast, the team's debrief is about which assumption broke, not whether the forecast was right or wrong. *We hit week six rather than week four because the platform team's API change shipped late.* That conversation produces useful information for the next forecast — the team learns what kinds of assumptions tend to break, and the stakeholder learns where the actual sources of slip are coming from. Within a quarter or two, the team is having a different kind of estimation conversation entirely: less about predicting, more about managing dependencies and assumptions explicitly.

The next chapter is about spikes — the move you reach for when *I don't know* is the honest answer and you need to convert it into a forecast you can defend. Most teams use spikes badly when they use them at all; they treat them as undirected exploration rather than the time-boxed investigations they're supposed to be. The chapter is about how to run spikes that produce decisions instead of more questions.

Chapter 11: Spikes

A spike is what you do when the work can't move until a question is answered.

Refinement is usually where the trigger shows up: a card the team can't scope — not because nobody has thought about it, but because scoping it needs a fact nobody currently has. Estimation produces the other version — work the team genuinely can't forecast. Chapter 10 pointed straight here: the spike is what turns an honest *we don't know* into something a stakeholder can plan around.

A spike is the named, bounded move for *we need to go and find out.* It is a time-boxed investigation, and its only product is a decision — or enough information for someone to make one.

That last part is the whole chapter. A spike does not build the thing. It does not produce a feature, half a feature, or a polished prototype anyone keeps. It produces knowledge — the specific knowledge a blocked decision is waiting on. The most common way teams ruin spikes is to let them quietly become the work: a developer is handed a vague spike, starts building, and three days later there is some half-built code and still no clean decision. A spike that ends in more code instead of a decision has missed its only job.

When you actually need one

Not every unknown is a spike. Most aren't.

A spike is for a question that only genuine investigation can answer — someone has to go and find something out by doing, not by discussing. Does this third-party API actually return what its documentation claims? How does the legacy billing system behave when two payments land in the same second? Will the new library hold up under the load we'd put through it? Questions like those can't be settled in a refinement conversation, however long it runs. Somebody has to go and look.

The unknown isn't always technical. Sometimes the ground that isn't solid is the requirement itself. The team is about to build on a stack of assumptions about what is actually needed, none of them checked — the card records what someone *thinks* the system should do, and no refinement conversation can turn that into shared understanding, because the understanding doesn't exist yet. There is only speculation. That is spike territory too. A spike can go and replace the speculation with fact — validate the assumptions against the real system, the real users, the real third-party behaviour — before the team commits a sprint to building on top of them.

That said, there is a line. If the team can resolve the question by talking it through for twenty minutes, or by one person reading a document for half an hour, it isn't a spike — it's part of the work, and it stays on the original card. Minor research belongs inside the story. Promoting every small uncertainty to a spike just litters the board with investigation cards and quietly teaches the team that "I'm not sure" is a reason to stop.

A spike is also not the place to settle a *should-we* question. Whether a feature is worth building is a product decision, and it belongs with whoever owns that call. A spike answers questions of fact and feasibility — can this be done, how, and at what cost — so the decision-owner can then make the decision well. The spike equips the decision. It doesn't make it.

When ready work becomes unfit

So far, this chapter has treated the decision to spike as something you make up front — at refinement, when a card can't be scoped, or in the face of work you can't forecast. Most of the time, that is where it happens. But not always, and the exception is worth its own section.

We once inherited a legacy system — old code, libraries five or six versions behind. The work in front of us was a library upgrade. We estimated it at three points, which for that team meant roughly three days, because a library upgrade is a known quantity: you bump the version, you fix what the compiler complains about, you ship.

Three days in, it was clear it would take longer. The stakeholder — this was a security upgrade, and they wanted it done — backed us to carry on to the end of the sprint. Then it rolled over: we had found that other libraries needed to move at the same time. The next sprint it rolled again, because the version bumps were causing breaking changes in code that several of those libraries all touched. What had been estimated as a library upgrade was now a refactor of most of the system.

We were lucky in one way — the stakeholder wanted the security holes closed regardless of cost, so nobody came after the three-point estimate. But the estimate was never the real problem. The real problem was that nobody had ever *decided* to refactor a large, ageing system with not much shelf life left in it — and refactoring a system that is on its way out is, most of the time, money set on fire. That decision got made by accident, one rollover at a time, because the work had been picked up as a three-day card and nobody stopped to ask whether the thing it had turned into was worth doing at all.

It is tempting to file this under bad estimation. But the deeper failure was a missing spike. The moment of the first rollover — the moment the work revealed it was not what the card said — the honest move was to stop building, say so at the standup, and raise a spike. The spike would have produced a dependency map and a set of costed options: full refactor, minimal security patching, or accelerated decommissioning. Three real choices for the stakeholder to make — instead of a refactor nobody chose, discovered three sprints deep.

A card can pass refinement honestly. Everyone can describe what done looks like; the card can look completely ready. And then the work itself, once underway, turns up something no refinement conversation could have surfaced — because the team did not know enough to know the question was there. I tell developers to imagine fixing the problem before they start, and it is good advice, but it has a hard limit: you cannot imagine the part of the problem you do not yet know exists.

So the discipline is about the moment of discovery. When work that was genuinely believed ready reveals, mid-flight, that it is not — that it is unscoped, or larger in kind and not merely in size — that is a spike trigger, every bit as much as anything caught at refinement. The signal is easy to name: you have stopped building and started finding out. The moment the work has turned into finding-out, stop calling it the work. Raise it, and spike it.

The question comes first

The single discipline that separates a useful spike from three wasted days: write the question down before the spike starts, and write the decision that's waiting on it.

A spike without a precise question is just unbounded research. It expands to fill whatever time it is given and ends with "we learned a lot" and nothing anyone can act on. *Spike the payments integration* is not a spike — it has no question, so the developer will simply start building the integration, and the spike has become the work before it began. Compare: *can the payments provider refund part of a charge, and does that need the original transaction ID? We need this to know whether the refund feature is one card or four.* That has a question, and it names the decision.

Sharpen the question into acceptance criteria — the specific things the spike has to be able to answer before it is done. *We can state whether partial refunds are supported. We can state whether they need the original transaction ID. We can state roughly what each option would cost to build.* Acceptance criteria do for a spike what they do for any other card: they make "done" a fact rather than a feeling, and they tell whoever picks the spike up exactly what they are being asked to come back with.

The quick test, before any of that detail: if you can't state the spike's question and the decision it unblocks in two sentences, you don't have a spike. You have unscoped work wearing a spike's name — and it will behave like unscoped work, running long, drifting, and ending without a result.

The timebox

A spike is time-boxed — usually a day or two, rarely more than three.

The box does two jobs. The first is the familiar one: investigation has no natural end, there is always more you could learn, and work expands to fill whatever time it is given. Without a box, "let's look into it" quietly becomes a fortnight.

The second job matters more, and it is the one teams forget. The box is a rescue line. A spike is a descent into something the team doesn't understand yet — and, like abseiling into a cave of unknown depth, the most important piece of equipment is the agreement about when you climb back up. The timebox is that agreement. When it runs out, whoever ran the spike comes back to the surface and the team looks at what they have: did we learn what we needed? Do we know enough to make the decision now? Or have we found that the cave goes deeper than anyone thought — in which case the honest move is to revise what we're looking for, or to decide deliberately to resupply for a longer descent. That resurfacing isn't the spike failing. It is the spike working. The box is what guarantees it happens, instead of someone disappearing into an unknown for far longer than anyone intended.

For the same reason, a spike shouldn't go dark. Short check-ins with the team partway through — here's what we've found, here's what's still open — are the radio contact that lets the team course-correct while the timebox still has room in it, rather than after it's spent. A spike that surfaces only at the very end has thrown away every chance to be redirected while redirection still mattered.

And the box is what makes a spike easy to grant in the first place. A stakeholder or a PO can say yes to "two days to find out" without much hesitation. They cannot really say yes to "we'll look into it," because that has no end, and they know it.

Knowledge, not work

A spike's shape varies. Some go wide — surveying several possible approaches, sizing each, so the team can choose between them. Others go deep and narrow — drilling into one specific question, because that single unknown is the only thing blocking the decision. Which shape a spike takes depends entirely on what is being decided, and that judgment belongs to the team. There is no rule that a spike must be broad, and none that it must be narrow. There is only the decision it exists to unblock, and the shape that answers it most directly.

What does not vary is what a spike produces. A spike produces knowledge — never a deliverable. Whatever code it generates along the way is a probe: it exists to answer the question, and it is usually thrown away. This is the line that keeps a spike honest. The moment a spike starts producing work the team intends to keep, it has stopped being a spike and become the work — done carelessly and half-finished — under a name that shielded it from scrutiny.

So the question to keep asking, all the way through a spike, is simply: *are we acquiring knowledge, or are we building?* The first is the spike doing its job. The second is the spike quietly failing at it.

The written outcome

A spike ends with a short written outcome. Not a verbal "yeah, it'll be fine" in a standup — a few lines, written down, that the team and the decision-owner can actually use.

A simple frame keeps the write-up honest: goal, assumptions, options, outcome. The goal is the question and the decision it unblocks. The assumptions are what the investigation took as given — the things that, if wrong, would change the answer. The options are the paths found, with their costs and risks. The outcome is the recommendation. A few honest sentences under each is enough; a spike's write-up should take minutes to read.

The non-negotiable part is the outcome. A spike ends in a recommendation or a decision — not in more questions. Even when the finding is bad news, it resolves to something actionable: *this is larger than we assumed; here are the three options and what each costs; the decision-owner needs to pick.* If the three options turn out to be questions that need further investigation, the spike has still done its job when it names what happens next — *we recommend a two-week discovery to answer them in sequence, starting with X, because that unblocks the roadmap.* That is still a decision-shaped result. What a spike must not end with is an unbounded pile of questions and no recommendation about which one to answer first, or a vague "we should look into it more." If the investigation genuinely uncovered that the real question is a different one, that is a legitimate result — but only when the new question is named and specific enough to stand as a spike in its own right.

Write it down, because the value of a spike is knowledge, and undocumented knowledge evaporates. The same depreciation that turns a refined card stale, back in chapter 7, turns an unwritten spike into three days nobody can find the result of.

Failure modes

Three patterns to watch for.

The spike becomes the work. No precise question, so the developer just starts building — tries something, it half-works, gets reported as progress at the standup, and the team presses on. Three days later there is half a feature, built exploratorily and therefore badly, and the question the spike was meant to answer is buried somewhere underneath it. Even if the thing ships, nobody can say whether the approach was the right one, because nobody ever answered the question — the team gambled rather than decided. The fix is upstream: the question and the decision it unblocks, written before the spike starts. If you can't write them, what you have isn't a spike, and calling it one only hides that it was never scoped.

The spike has no endpoint. It is open-ended research. It runs past its box, or it ends with "we learned a lot" and no recommendation anyone can act on. The fix is the timebox, actually enforced, and the rule that a spike ends in a written outcome. A spike that has produced no recommendation when its box runs out hasn't finished early — it has failed, and the team should look at why, because usually the question was vague.

Spikes multiply without a boundary. One spike ends by revealing the need for another, and that one reveals a third. This is not, by itself, a failure — often it is the spike doing its job, telling the team that the area is genuinely larger and less understood than anyone assumed. The pragmatic response is to stop and name it: if a single question has unravelled into a whole territory of them, what the team has actually discovered is the need for a *discovery* — a deliberately bounded body of investigation, a planned set of spikes with one overall goal, one timebox, and one decision point at the end. The failure is only the unbounded version: spikes spawning spikes with no consolidation and no decision ever made, investigation becoming a permanent state the team lives in rather than a thing it does and finishes. The fix is the boundary. One spike or a whole discovery, the work has a timebox and a point at which the team commits to deciding with what it has.

The rescue, in week one

Teams you inherit tend to fail at spikes in one of two opposite ways.

The first team never spikes. It meets an unknown and just starts building, then discovers the problem halfway through the sprint, when the cost of being wrong is highest. For this team, the move is to make the spike visible. When refinement turns up a card that genuinely can't be scoped because of a missing fact, name the spike out loud, write its question and its timebox, and put it on the board as its own piece of work. You aren't adding ceremony — you are pulling a risk that was going to surface mid-sprint forward into a bounded, cheap investigation.

The second team spikes everything, and the spikes are undirected research that never ends. For this team, the move is to enforce the question and the written outcome. The next spike the team runs, don't let it start until its question and the decision it unblocks are written on the card. End it when the box runs out. Make whoever ran it write the outcome — goal, assumptions, options, recommendation — and bring it back to the team. The first time a spike ends in a clean decision instead of a shrug, the team feels the difference.

The signal that the rescue has taken is the same in both directions: spikes start ending in decisions, and the team stops being ambushed mid-sprint by unknowns it should have investigated first.

That closes Part 2. The one-on-one, the standup, planning, refinement, the retro, the demo, estimation, the spike — eight feedback loops, eight places where a team turns information into a decision and the work moves on. Some run with the whole team, one runs one person at a time, and one runs with the people outside the team altogether; what they share is that each is a point where information goes in and a decision comes out. A framework only guarantees the loops exist; whether they do any good depends entirely on the thinking the team brings to them. Run with that thinking, they are the difference between a team that delivers and a team that is merely busy. Run as rituals — performed because the calendar says so, with the thinking left out — they are the overhead that gave “agile” its bad name.

Part 3 turns from the ceremonies to the repairs: the specific, cheap, fast fixes for the dysfunctions that show up, in some form, in almost every team you will ever inherit.

Part Three: The Cheap Fixes

Every fix in this part is cheap. Not one of them needs a budget, a new tool, a headcount request, or anyone's sign-off. They cost a decision, a conversation, or a column on a board. That is their great advantage. It is also the reason most teams never make them.

A fix with a price tag has a sponsor. Someone has to approve the spend, so someone owns it, so it goes on a roadmap and gets a name and a status update. A free fix has none of that. It surfaces as "we should really..." near the end of a retro, everyone nods, and nothing happens, because there is no budget line to defend and nobody whose job it is to see it through. The cheapest fixes have the worst odds of being made. A team can know exactly what is wrong with how its work flows and still not change it for years — not because the fix is hard, but because the fix is free, and free things drift.

Part 1 was about seeing the system and finding the constraint. Part 2 was about the ceremonies — the feedback loops, run with intention rather than by rote. This part is about what happens between the loops: the work itself, and whether it moves. A team can run flawless ceremonies and still watch its work crawl, because the ceremonies are where the team thinks and the flow is where the work lives, and the two are not the same thing.

Think back to the five patterns from the diagnosis — the status standup, the decision graveyard, the sign-off chokepoint, the escalation reflex, the recycled retro. Two of them were ceremony problems, and Part 2 dealt with them. The other three are not about meetings at all. They are about work sitting still: a backlog of decisions nobody will make, a queue behind one overloaded person, a clarification stuck somewhere over the team's head. That is what this part rescues. And it rescues all of it the same way, because all of it has the same cause. Work is not waiting on code. It is waiting on a decision. Accumulated across weeks, unmade decisions become what this part calls decision debt, and the chapters that follow attack it in each place it piles up: inside the columns, in the cadence, past the end of the board, and in the backlog.

The last chapter of the part turns from the work to the people around it. Some of the decisions a team waits on are not the team's to make and not even inside the team's own organisation — they sit with a stakeholder, a sponsor, a customer who has to test before anything can ship. The same decision-debt lens applies, but the fix is less about a column on a board and more about who you keep in the loop, and how. It is still cheap. It still costs a conversation rather than a budget. It is just that the conversation is with someone who can stop you.

This is why the fixes can be cheap. If the constraint were genuinely resources — too few engineers, too little compute, a missing capability — then money would be the answer and there would be nothing cheap about it. But the constraint is rarely resources. It is decisions queued, deferred, or routed through someone who has not got to them yet. You do not need a budget to make a decision happen sooner. You need to see where the decisions are stuck and change something small so they stop being stuck. Small is the whole point. The lightest move that produces the largest change — that was the principle in Part 1, and this is the part where you finally get to make the move.

The lens for the part is flow. Not flow as a feeling, and not flow as a branded methodology — flow in the plain sense: work moving steadily from started to finished, without long stretches of sitting still. Most teams have no real picture of their own flow. They can tell you how busy everyone is. They cannot tell you how long a piece of work actually takes from the moment someone starts it to the moment it ships, or how much of that time was spent waiting rather than being worked on. When you measure it, the ratio is brutal and consistent: most work, most of the time, is waiting. The cheap fixes are the moves that take the waiting out.

Each chapter that follows is one cheap fix for one way work stops moving. Too much started and nothing finished. A constraint with a name and a calendar. A team that has lost the habit of deciding. A backlog that is really a graveyard. The people outside the team whose unmade decisions stop the work cold. None of them will cost you anything to try. Each of them will be resisted, quietly, by a system that has arranged itself around the problem and finds the problem more comfortable than the change. That resistance is not a reason the fixes do not work. It is the reason they have to be made deliberately, by someone whose job it is to see them through. That someone is you.

Chapter 12: The Process You Actually Have

Ask a team to describe how their work flows and they will point at the board. Three or four columns, usually: to do, in progress, sometimes a review step, done. Then watch the work itself for a week and count the stages a card actually passes through. It will not be three. It will rarely be four.

The board shows the process someone set up once — often before half the current team arrived — and the work has been quietly diverging from it ever since. Stages appear that were never drawn. A card a developer considers finished sits somewhere, untouched, waiting for a tester to look at it. There is no column for that waiting, so it happens inside "in progress" or "done", invisibly, and nobody can say how long it lasts. The board is not lying out of malice. It is lying because the work moved and the board did not.

This chapter is one exercise that fixes that. It is about as cheap as an intervention gets — an hour with the team — and it is the one I run first with almost every team, because you cannot improve a flow you cannot see, and most teams cannot see their own.

The exercise

Here is the whole of it. Get the team in front of the board. Go to the leftmost column and ask two questions. First: what has to be true for a card to be allowed *into* this column? Second: what has to happen before it can move to the *next* one? Write the answers up beside each column. Then move right and do it again, column by column, to the end of the board.

That is the exercise. Two questions, per column, asked out loud, with the team. It takes about an hour. Do it however your team already works — a board you all click into, or a wall with sticky notes if that is still you. The medium does not matter. What matters is that the team answers, not you.

Everything else in this chapter is about what those two questions drag into the light, and how to run the hour so that the team, not you, does the seeing.

What the board is hiding

The two questions are simple. The answers are not, because the team has never had to say them out loud together before.

You will reach a column boundary — most often the one around testing — ask what has to happen for a card to cross it, and the answers will not agree. One developer says testing happens before the review. Another says after. A third says it is obvious — testing starts when the dev work is finished. The tester, who has not spoken yet, will say quietly that he often does not actually know when something is ready for him, because nobody tells him consistently.

That moment is the exercise working. The board had one quiet boundary, but underneath it the team had been running on three or four different mental models of when work moved to the next person, and had been for as long as anyone could remember. The board never forced the disagreement into the open, because a board never does. It just shows whatever columns it has and lets each person fill the gaps with their own assumption. The work paid for that quiet disagreement every day, and nobody ever saw the bill.

What the disagreement exposes is a *handoff* — a point where work passes from one person, or one role, to another. The card leaves the developer and goes to the tester. And here is the part worth slowing down for, because it is the whole reason this exercise belongs in this book: at a handoff, work stops. Not because anyone is slacking. It stops because the next person has to notice the card is there, decide it is their turn, and decide it is genuinely ready for them. Until those decisions are made, the card sits.

That sitting is the most expensive thing on most boards, and it is invisible, because there is no column for it. A developer finishes, slides the card to the next column, and feels finished. The card is not finished. It is waiting — not on work, on a decision: the tester's decision to pick it up. A hidden stage is not a tidiness problem. It is decision debt — accumulated, untracked, unowned.

This is what mapping the board is really for. Not a neater board — a visible one. Every column you are missing is a place where work waits on a decision, untracked and unowned. The exercise makes those places appear, so you can see them, measure them, and give them a name. Once a stage has a name and a column you can put a time against it, which is the next chapter, and you can start asking why the time is what it is. None of that is possible while the stage is hidden inside another column.

The argument is the point

Most of the value of this hour is not the map. It is the argument.

When the team discovers it has been running on three or four different mental models of the same handoff, it will argue about which one is right. Let it. Do not step in and rule. The argument is the team doing out loud, and together, a piece of thinking each of them has been avoiding alone for years. A developer hears, properly, what the tester has been waiting on and what "ready" actually means to him. The tester hears why the developers have been doing things in the order they have. They are not really arguing about a column. They are discovering that they have been quietly miscommunicating the whole time — and that a great deal of the rework and friction each of them had privately blamed on the others was nobody's fault. The gap was always in the board, not in the people.

You will know the exercise has landed when someone says some version of: "oh — so I thought you'd picked that up, and you thought I still had it." That sentence is worth more than the board you redraw afterwards. The redrawn board is just where the realisation gets written down.

So when the argument starts, your job is not to settle it. It is to keep it honest and keep it moving: make sure the quieter people are heard, keep it about the work rather than personalities, and see that it ends in a definition the whole team will actually use. The definition is theirs. You only held the room while they found it.

Ask, don't tell

This is the first exercise in this part of the book, so it is worth being plain about how to run it, because the same method runs all of them.

You do not walk up to the board and announce what is wrong with it. You will often see what is wrong within a minute — that is not the point. Tell the team their board is broken and you have produced a fact, which they will nod at and forget. Let the team work it out and you have produced a change. The method, here and in every exercise that follows, is a ladder, and you climb only as far as you have to.

The first rung is to ask. The two questions are the asking. Most of the time, asking is enough: the team starts answering, the answers collide, and the team sees the gap without your ever having named it. You stay on this rung as long as it is working.

The second rung, if asking stalls — if the team insists the board is fine and the answers all suspiciously agree — is an anecdote. You tell a story that carries the shape of the problem without being about them, and you let them make the connection themselves. For handoffs I tend to reach for the relay race: a four-by-one-hundred relay is won and lost in the handoff zones, not in the running, and teams with faster runners lose finals every year because somebody fumbled a baton. Then you go quiet and let the team look at their own board and find their own baton. The anecdote is a mirror; you hold it up, you do not explain the reflection.

The third rung, and the last resort, is show-and-tell. If the anecdote does not land, you make the hidden stage physically visible. Take a real card — the one everyone agrees was finished last Tuesday and shipped on Friday — and ask the team to walk you through where it actually was on each of those days. Somewhere in that walk there will be a day, or three, the card spent in no column at all. Mark it there. Ask the team what to call it. By the time they have named it, the realisation is theirs; you only made the space for it.

You will rarely need the third rung. But run the ladder in order, every time, and never start higher than you must. The further down the ladder the team gets there on its own, the more the fix belongs to them — and a fix that belongs to the team is the only kind that survives you leaving the room.

The fix

Mapping the board produces two fixes, and they are different sizes.

The small one is immediate: draw the real process. Wherever the team has just discovered a stage that cards genuinely wait in — between development and test, before a product owner's sign-off, wherever it turns out to be — that stage gets a column. Not because more columns are better, but because a stage you can see is a stage you can manage, and a stage you cannot see will quietly eat your weeks. The "ready for test" column the team swore it did not need is the clearest case. The team does not need the column because it is fond of columns. It needs it because the stage already exists. The only question was ever whether anyone could see it.

The larger fix is to attack the handoff itself, and this is where mapping the board stops being bookkeeping. A handoff costs you the wait on both sides of it. The card sitting in "ready for test" is the visible half. The tester then arriving at it completely cold — no context, rebuilding in their own head what the developer already had in theirs — is the other half. The cheapest way to shrink a handoff is to stop treating the two stages as strictly sequential. The tester does not have to wait for "done" to begin. Test cases can be written while the code is being written. The tester and the developer can be in conversation throughout, agreeing the edge cases before the code exists rather than after. The automated checks can be ready the day the code is. Done well, the card barely pauses at the handoff at all, because the next stage was already under way when it arrived.

That is the move — and notice it is not "eliminate the handoff". Some handoffs are real; a specialist is a specialist. The move is to overlap the work on either side of the handoff so that it stops being a full stop and becomes a comma.

When the board is fine

Sometimes you run this exercise and the board is fine.

The team answers the two questions and the answers agree. "Done" means the same thing to the developer, the tester, and the product owner. The columns match the stages the work genuinely passes through. The handoffs are tight, because the team already works the way the previous section described without anyone having told it to. This happens — usually with teams that have been together a long time and have already had, informally and over years, the argument this exercise forces into an hour.

When it happens, the exercise has not failed. It has told you something true and useful: this is not where your team's problem is. Say so, plainly — "your process is sound, we do not need to touch it" — and go and look elsewhere. A team does not need a new column, a new rule, or a new working agreement simply because you have arrived and feel you ought to leave a mark. The exercises in this book are for finding waste, not for manufacturing it. The most disciplined thing you can do with a sound process is recognise it and leave it alone.

There is also the matter of fit. A team of seasoned operators with strong communication may work perfectly well with three columns and no formal rules, because the structure they need has been built into how they already talk to each other. A team that is newer, less settled, or less inclined to own its own coordination probably cannot. The right amount of structure on a board is not a fixed answer. It is the amount the team needs to compensate for what its day-to-day communication does not already cover — no more. The exercises in this part are for finding out what the team actually needs, not for installing more of it.

This matters well beyond this one chapter. A delivery manager who always finds a problem teaches the team that the interventions are about the manager, not the work. A delivery manager who runs an exercise, finds nothing, and says so, earns the credibility that makes the next intervention land — the one where there really is something to fix.

The team that didn't need a column

I once had a team with four columns: to do, in progress, review, done. I knew it was not their real process before I had asked a single question. I had watched one standup, and the tester had spent most of it asking whether this thing or that thing was ready for him to pick up. If the board had been honest, he would not have had to ask. So I knew there was a handoff the team was not yet seeing on its board.

We sat down for a ways-of-working session and I had not finished introducing the exercise before a senior, outspoken developer told me they had four columns and that was all they needed. I asked him to tell me about the process. Then I asked the question I already knew was going to do the work: when does testing happen, and how does the tester know a card is ready for him to pick up?

The answers from the developers came fast and did not agree. Testing happens before review. Testing happens after review. It is obvious when something is ready for test — it is once the dev work is finished. There were three confident answers and they were three different processes. The tester, who had been quiet, spoke up softly and said he often did not know when things were ready, because nobody told him consistently. And then — the more revealing thing — he said he was often conflicted about which item to test next, because there was no agreed priority and he had to guess, or constantly ask the tech lead.

Laid bare in about five minutes: the whole team had been running on four different mental models of when work moved to the tester, and the tester had been sitting in the gap between them, guessing.

I suggested we put a "ready for test" column on the board. The developers were not happy. The senior, outspoken one just kept saying "no". Flatly — the same word, said again, said again, said again. He had decided no was the answer before I had finished asking the question. The rest of the team's complaint was more articulate but landed in the same place: I was overcomplicating their nice clean board. I said the board should look like the process — and the process plainly had a stage where work sat waiting to be tested, whether they wanted to draw it or not. I offered them a way out: try it for a sprint or two, and if it makes things worse, revert.

We ended up adding two columns, "ready for test" and "in test", with a rule that the ready-for-test column was kept in priority order so the tester would never have to guess what to pick up next. Then I asked when the team should communicate that a card had moved to ready for test. Half of them said standup; one said "when it's ready". The team eventually settled on a note in the team channel the moment a card crossed into ready for test.

The part that mattered most happened after the exercise officially ended. Within a few weeks the same team had started seeing the other places its board was hiding work — tickets that were technically "in review" but had been waiting on a reviewer for days, work that had been called done but was sitting waiting on a stakeholder to confirm. The hour we spent finding one hidden stage taught them to look for the others themselves. That is the thing about this exercise that is hard to see at the time. The first hidden column you name with the team is not really about that column. It is about the team learning to notice gaps it had stopped seeing.

Three ways it goes wrong

The first is that you map the board, redraw it accurately, and a month later it has drifted back. The new columns are not being updated; the team has quietly gone back to moving cards the old way. That means the exercise produced a diagram but not a change. The board is the team's tool or it is nothing — if the team will not use the map, the mapping did not reach the thing that was actually wrong, and you have more work to do, most likely about whether the board is the team's instrument or the manager's.

The second is over-correction. The team finds one hidden stage, gets enthusiastic, and now every micro-step is a column and the board has fourteen of them. A board with fourteen columns is its own bureaucracy, and it is no more honest than the three-column one — it just lies in the other direction, implying a precision the work does not have. The test for a column is not "is this a step" but "is this a place where work genuinely waits, long enough and often enough that we need to see it". Work that flies through a stage without stopping does not need a column.

The third is the one that is your fault. You see the problem early — you usually will — map the board *for* the team, present them with the corrected version, and feel efficient. You have produced your board. It will drift back faster than anything, because the team never had the argument, never reached the realisation, and has no reason to defend a map it did not draw. The hour the team spends arguing is not the slow way to run this exercise. It is the exercise.

The rescue

If you suspect your board is lying to you — and if it has three or four columns while your work plainly moves through more stages than that, it is — you do not need a project to fix it. You need an hour and the team looking at the board together.

Go to the board. Ask, of each column, what gets a card in and what gets it out. Write down what they say. Let the disagreement happen, and do not rush it, because the disagreement is the team finding the stages the board has hidden and the words it has blurred. By the end of the hour you will have the process the team actually runs, drawn where everyone can see it. And seeing it is the whole prerequisite for the rest of this part of the book. You cannot put a time against a stage you have not named. You cannot shrink a handoff you will not admit exists.

The board is not a status report you keep for someone above you. It is the team's picture of its own work — and the only picture worth having is one that tells the truth.

Chapter 13: Where the Time Goes

A team that has just mapped its board, properly, knows the shape of its process. It does not yet know the speed of it. The map shows you the stages. It does not show you which one of them is eating your weeks.

That is the next question, and it is the one most teams have never sat down to answer. Ask a team how long a piece of work takes to get from start to finish and you will get answers that range from "a few days" to "depends on the work" — neither of which is a number. Ask them how much of that time is spent doing the work, versus waiting for someone to pick it up, and you will get nothing at all. Most teams do not know. They have never had reason to find out.

This chapter is the exercise that finds out. It is cheaper than chapter 12 — half an hour, you can do it inside a standup if you have to — and what it reveals is almost always the same: most of your cycle time is waiting, not working, and the team had no idea by how much.

The exercise

Get the team in front of the board. For each column, ask two questions. First: how long does a card currently sit in this column, on average? Second: how long should it sit in this column? Write both numbers up next to the column. Then move to the next column and do it again. At the end, add up the "currently" column. That total is your cycle time.

That is the exercise. Two questions per column, asked of the people who actually move the cards. Five minutes if the team is honest, ten if they argue. You can do it in whatever tool your team uses, on a whiteboard, in a doc, on the back of an envelope — none of that matters. The numbers do not have to be precise. They are not a study. They are the team's best honest estimate, and the team's best honest estimate is what you want, because it is what the team will defend or change later.

The rest of this chapter is about why those two questions do what they do, and how to run the half hour when the team — or one person on it — does not want to.

What the numbers reveal

The first thing you will see is the gap.

For most columns, the team will name a "currently" that is meaningfully larger than the "should" — sometimes by a factor of three or four, sometimes by an order of magnitude. The "ready for review" column that should sit at half a day sits at two days. The "in test" column that should be a day is four. The card that the team genuinely worked on for six hours has been on the board for nine days, and the gap is in places where, by anyone's standard, nothing was supposed to be happening.

That gap is the chapter, and there is one thing worth slowing down for, because it is the whole reason the exercise belongs in this book. The big numbers are almost never in the columns where the work happens. They are in the columns where the work waits. Cards do not pile up on the developers because they are slow. They pile up in front of the reviewer, the tester, the product owner, the security checker — anywhere the work needs to be picked up by someone else. And what is the work doing in those columns? It is not being worked on. It is waiting for someone to notice it, decide it is their turn, and decide it is ready. The exact same problem as the last chapter, in a new disguise. Hidden stages were decision debt you could not see. Long columns are decision debt you can see and have not weighed.

That is what the two questions force into the light. The "currently" number is the size of a queue. The "should" number is the size the team thinks the queue ought to be. The gap between them is your improvement target, and the gap is almost always made of waiting.

Knowing this changes what you do next, and it should. A team that thinks its cycle time is too long usually tries to make people work faster. It is almost always the wrong move. Working faster shaves a few hours off a column the team only spends a few hours in. Killing the waiting in a column that sits at five days saves five days. The same effort, applied to the column where the work waits, returns ten or twenty times the result. That is what "cheap fix" actually means in this book — not that the move is small, but that the move is in the right column.

"Can you really tell me this will get done?"

Half the time you will run this exercise and the team will be willing. The other half, someone will not be — usually the most senior person in the room, usually a tech lead or a staff developer, usually the one who is impatient about the meeting eating their work time. They will say so out loud. "I can't see the point of this. I just want to get back to work."

There is a question that converts them, and it is worth keeping in your back pocket because you will need it more than once. You ask: you have committed to delivering this list of stories in this sprint, and there are stakeholders waiting on that work — can you tell me, based on your current workflow, that this is actually going to get done?

The honest answer is almost never yes. The honest answer is "we'll do our best, but we can't guarantee." That is not a yes. That is a person admitting they are about to break a promise and asking you to accept the breakage in advance. You do not have to argue with them. You just point at their own board and ask: why can't you give a rough estimate? The process is mapped out here. Five minutes — can you spare five minutes to find out whether your commitment is real?

The answer to that question is yes about nineteen times out of twenty, because the alternative — refusing to spend five minutes checking whether a promise is keepable — is a position that does not survive being said out loud. The tech lead sits down. The exercise begins.

The conversion move is not aggression. It is consent. You are not telling the tech lead the exercise is important; you are letting him discover that his own commitment depends on it.

The conversation moves from "this is wasting my time" to "I had better know whether the answer to my own question is yes." That is the same move from the last chapter, with a different lever. Ask, do not tell — and where you can, ask in a way that makes the case for the exercise itself impossible to refuse.

Easy columns first

When the team is doing the numbers, do not start with the column you suspect is the worst. Start with the obvious-waste ones — the ready-for-review queue, the in-review column, anywhere work plainly waits for someone other than the person who finished it. These columns are easy for two reasons. First, the team mostly agrees the "should" number is small or zero — nobody seriously argues that work should sit in a review queue for three days. Second, nobody in the room owns the queue, so nobody has to defend it. The numbers go up, the team nods, the gap is named, and the room has agreed on a finding before any politics has been spent.

Now the hard columns are easier. The chokepoint column — the one where work waits on a single overloaded person who happens to be in the room — has lost its defenders, because the team has just agreed that big "currently" numbers are a problem in general, and the chokepoint's number is the biggest one on the board. The owner of the chokepoint is rarely the worst person in the room about this. They are usually the most relieved, because the queue in front of them was something they could feel but could not name, and the exercise has just named it on a wall for everyone to share.

The order matters. Start with the politics-free columns. Build agreement on the shape of the problem. Then go to the column the team has been quietly building its workflow around, and find that the room is already on your side.

The 0-days trap

When the team gets to a column like "in review" and you ask what the "should" number is, you will get answers like "one day", "two days", "I don't know." Do not let the conversation settle there. Ask the room: who wants to know what the right answer is?

The right answer is zero. Not because review is bad — review is necessary, and a team that ships unreviewed code is going to ship a different kind of disaster — but because the time a card spends *waiting* in the review queue is not the same thing as the time it spends being reviewed. The review itself takes minutes. The wait for someone to start the review takes days. The first is a step in the process. The second is the work sitting there while the process does nothing.

This distinction matters and it has to be drawn cleanly, because a reader who hears "review is waste" will conclude they should skip code review, and they would be wrong. The review is necessary and not negotiable. The *queue around the review* is the waste. The fix is not "stop reviewing"; it is "stop waiting to review." Cards in the review queue are decision-waiting again, the decision being "I will pick this up now." A team can attack that wait in several ways — a reviewer rota, a cap on how many cards the queue is allowed to hold, a signal in the team channel the moment a card is ready, the same way the team in chapter 12 dealt with the ready-for-test queue. The goal is not zero review. The goal is zero wait.

The same logic applies anywhere there is a queue in front of a step the customer does not directly value but the team cannot skip. Sign-off. Security review. Compliance check. All of them are necessary. None of the queues in front of them are.

The fix

The fix from this exercise is rarely "all of the columns get attacked at once." That is the version of the move that takes six weeks to implement and never finishes. The fix is the one chapter 1 has been promising — the lightest move that produces the largest change. You take the biggest gap on the board between "currently" and "should" — almost always one of the queues — and you do one thing to it. Just one. Cap how many cards can sit in the column at once. Set up a reviewer rota. Agree the team-channel signal. Run it for a sprint. Measure it again. If the gap closed, you have your evidence that the lever you pulled was the right one. If it did not, you have evidence the lever was somewhere else, and the cost was one sprint.

You will be tempted, sometimes, to fix several columns at once, especially when the team is energised by what they have just seen. Resist. Two interventions running at once means you cannot tell which one worked, and a team that cannot tell which intervention worked loses faith in the next round.

The other temptation, the more dangerous one, is to take the numbers and run them upstairs. "Look how much waste we have!" Do not do this either, at least not without warning the team. The exercise produces an honest set of numbers about the team, and honesty about the team belongs first to the team. If those numbers get used as a stick by someone above the team, the next time you ask the question the team will give you the answers it thinks are safe, and you have lost the instrument. The exercise is an internal mirror, not an external report card.

What this does for planning

There is one more thing the numbers give you, and it is worth naming because it is what makes the next planning session honest. Once a team knows how long each column actually takes, "can we commit to this list of work in this sprint?" stops being a guess. You add up the cycle time of the work proposed against the sprint length, and either the answer is yes or it is no. The conversation about which items to cut, or which column to attack, or whether to run more in parallel this time, happens before the commitment is made — not afterwards as an apology. Chapter 10 argued that forecasts have to account for waiting. This is the chapter where the team finally has the numbers to do it.

When the numbers are fine

It happens, sometimes, that you run this exercise and the gaps are small.

The "currently" and "should" numbers are within shouting distance of each other for every column. The team has, somehow — through history, through luck, through the kind of long apprenticeship the previous chapter's edge case described — already arranged its work so that things do not sit very long anywhere. When that happens, recognise it and stop. Tell the team plainly: "your cycle time is roughly what it should be — there is not a flow problem here, and there is not a queue we need to fix." Then go and look elsewhere. The problem is in another room.

This is the same discipline as the last chapter, and it bears repeating because it gets harder, not easier, as the book goes on. Each new exercise is a new way you might feel you should leave a mark. Each new exercise can come up empty, and an empty result is a real finding. A delivery manager who can run an exercise and walk away from it with nothing to do has more credibility than one who manufactures a project out of every number.

The 10-day promise

I once ran this with a team in the middle of a sprint, with stakeholders waiting on the work.

I had explained the exercise for about a minute when an outspoken tech lead said he could not see the point of it. He wanted to get back to work; the session was eating his work time. I said he could go back to work as soon as he could answer one question for me. He had committed to delivering this list of stories in this sprint, and stakeholders were waiting on the work. Could he really tell me, based on the team's current workflow, that this would actually get done?

He said what people in his position always say. "We'll do our best to get through all of this, but we can't guarantee."

I said: why can't you give a rough estimate? Your process is mapped out here. What if we spitballed it together for five minutes? Could you spare five minutes?

He said "OK."

We went through each column. How long does it currently sit here? How long should it? The numbers were not anything special — a day in to-do, a day in in-progress, the usual — until we totalled them up. Ten days. The total time, from a card entering the board to a card leaving the board, was ten days. The promise the team had made was to ship a story inside a week.

The room went quiet. Everyone went quiet. Dead silent. The tech lead's face changed in a way you do not see often in a meeting room.

I worked the easy ones first. "Ready for review" — how long should that sit? One day. Two days. I don't know. I asked the room: who wants to know what the right answer is? I told them: zero days. It is complete waste. Customers do not get value from how long a card waits to be reviewed. They do not even know it sat there. You cannot skip the review itself — that is your quality work and you need it — but the *wait* is non-value-adding to anyone. So what should you do? A junior developer, who had not spoken yet, said: "Review it as soon as it is up. As efficiently as possible." I said: there you go. You have just cut between one and three days out of your process. The promise you made to ship a story in a week is actually achievable. It just was not achievable with your old ten-day board.

The tech lead stayed for the rest of the session. He did not say a great deal — he did not need to. The numbers had said everything they needed to.

Three ways it goes wrong

The first is that the team treats the numbers as a benchmark and gets defensive. The "currently" column starts being negotiated downward, away from the truth, because the team thinks they are being measured. You have to draw the line up front: the numbers are the team's, the team is allowed to be wrong, and nothing said in this exercise leaves this room. If you cannot say that honestly, do not run the exercise — find a different intervention — because dishonest numbers are worse than no numbers.

The second is that the team fixes every column at once and loses the ability to learn from the result. Pick one column, fix one thing, run a sprint, measure again. The exercise is not just an inventory of problems; it is a baseline you can re-measure. Many small evidence-bearing experiments are worth more than one big undirected reorganisation.

The third is mistaking busyness for cycle time. A team can be very, very busy and still have terrible cycle time, because most of the time is waiting and not working. When someone in the room says "we just need to work harder" or "we just need more capacity", look back at the columns. If the big gaps are in queues — and they nearly always are — more hours of work into the busy columns will not move them. The fix is in a column where nobody is currently typing.

The rescue

If you do not know what your team's cycle time is, or worse if you know it is too long and you do not know which column is to blame, you do not need a measurement project. You need half an hour, the team, and the two questions.

Get the team to the board. For each column, ask how long a card sits in there now, and how long it should. Write both numbers up. Total the "now" column. The total will surprise you, and the gap between the now and the should, somewhere on the board, will be enormous. Pick the worst gap. Do one cheap thing about it. Run a sprint. Come back and measure again.

You will not need to do this many times before the team is volunteering to run it themselves. That is the point at which the exercise has done its real work — not the times getting smaller, but the team being the thing that gets the times smaller.

Chapter 14: Where Done Really Is

A team that has just measured its cycle time knows how long work takes inside its board. It does not yet know whether what it is calling "done" is really done.

That is the next question. Ask a team, after a sprint review, how many stories they finished, and you will get a number. Ask the customer, the same week, how many of those stories are doing work for them, and the number will be smaller — usually much smaller. Somewhere between the team's "done" column and the customer's experience there is a stretch of time and a sequence of steps the team does not measure, does not own, and often does not even draw on the board. That stretch is the chapter.

This chapter is the exercise that surfaces it. It is the cheapest of the three exercises so far — fifteen minutes, you can do it over a coffee — and what it produces is the part of "done" the team has been quietly not counting.

The exercise

Pick a story that the team called "done" in the last sprint. A specific one — the one closest to the date the team marked it done. Now walk through what happened to it from the moment it crossed the "done" line until the customer got value from it. List every step. Every wait, every sign-off, every deployment, every email asking someone to flip a switch. Put a rough time against each step.

That is the exercise. One card, one walk-through, fifteen minutes. The list at the end has two parts. First, every step the team's official "done" already covers — the things that have to be true before the team will move the card. Second, every step that happens after "done" but before the customer benefits. The second list is what this chapter is about.

The rest of this chapter is about why that second list usually exists, what the team does with it, and the related question of where the *start* of work — the definition of ready — really is.

What "done" usually hides

Most teams treat "done" as "the developer is finished." Some treat it as "the developer is finished and a tester has signed off." A few include "merged into the main branch." Each of these is a definition. Each of them stops short of the customer.

What sits in the gap depends on the team and the system, but the candidates are predictable. Code is merged but not deployed. Deployed but not released to the user. Released but waiting on a feature flag. Released but waiting on a stakeholder to verify it does what they said they wanted. Verified but waiting on a marketing communication, a support training, a sales enablement. Any one of these can take days. All of them together, on a single piece of work, can take longer than the work that produced the work.

And the team does not see it. The board does not show it, because the card has already moved past the last column. The cycle-time exercise from the last chapter did not catch it, because the cycle ended at the same place the board ended. Honest planning estimates are honest about the work *inside* the board, but the work *outside* the board is invisible.

Here is the part worth slowing down for, because it is the whole reason this exercise belongs in this book. Everything in that post-done list — the deployment that has not happened, the stakeholder who has not verified, the flag that has not been switched, the sign-off that has not been chased — is decision debt, accumulated past the end of the board where the team cannot see it. Sometimes it is a decision nobody has been asked to make. Sometimes it is a decision somebody has been asked to make and has not got to. Always it is the same shape as everything else in this part of the book: work waiting on a decision, not on more work. The hidden stages from chapter 12 were inside the board. The long columns from chapter 13 were inside the board. The hidden steps in this chapter are *past* the board, which is why the team has not been able to attack them — they cannot attack what they cannot see.

The argument again

The exercise will produce the same kind of argument the last two exercises did, with the same payoff, because it is the same disagreement at a different point in the flow.

You walk the team through the post-done list of one card and they will start to differ on what "done" should have meant in the first place. A developer says done is "merged." A tester says done is "tested in staging." A product owner says done is "live for users." A stakeholder, if there is one in the room, says done is "the thing it was meant to do is happening, in the customer's hands, and we have confirmed that." Each of them is right about their own definition. None of them has been speaking the same language.

When the team writes down what done has to mean — and they should, by the end of this exercise — it is rarely the longest possible version that wins. The longest possible version of done belongs to the stakeholder, and it is the customer's done, and the team mostly cannot control all of it. The version that wins is the longest version of done the team can genuinely commit to. The boundary is "what we can promise will be true before we call this finished." That boundary is real and the team can hold it. The work past that boundary is somebody else's, and the team's job is to make it visible — to draw the post-done steps on the board, even though they are not the team's columns, so the wait is somebody's job to chase.

The deliverable from the exercise is not a longer to-do list for the developers. It is a definition of done the team will stand behind, and a picture of what has to happen after that, owned by the people who can do something about it.

Ask, don't tell

The same ladder from chapter 12 runs here, slightly shorter because the team has done two of these exercises already.

The first rung is to ask. The two questions are: when did we say this was done, and when did the customer get value from it? Most teams will start answering and discover the gap in the first or second card. The first card is enough.

The second rung, if the team insists there is no gap, is to pick a card the customer has not actually used yet. Walk through where that card is now. If the card was called "done" three weeks ago and the customer cannot see it, the team will see the gap by the end of the walk-through.

The third rung is barely a third rung. If the team still cannot see it, ask the stakeholder. The stakeholder will see it, because the stakeholder is where it lives.

The other side: definition of ready

The same logic runs at the *start* of the work, and it is worth touching even though the chapter on refinement has covered most of it.

Work pulled into "in progress" before it is ready is the mirror image of work called "done" before it is finished. Both are decisions about a gate. Both, when fudged, produce a queue you can only see by where the cards eventually pile up. The card that was pulled too early ends up in a column waiting for an answer the team should have had before they started — a clarification, a design decision, an external dependency. It blocks, sometimes for days. The cost of pulling early is not paid at the pull; it is paid later, in a stage the team will not connect back to the pull unless somebody draws the line.

The exercise for the start gate is the same shape as the exercise for the end gate. Pick a card from the last sprint that ran into a block partway through. Walk back through it. When was the question that blocked it answerable? Was it answerable when the team pulled the card? If not, that is your definition-of-ready failure, and the line you write — the bar a card has to clear to enter progress — should include the thing that was missing.

This is one place the book genuinely repeats itself, and that is by design. The same decision-latency problem shows up at the front of the board, in the middle of the board, and past the end of the board, and the exercises for finding it look almost the same in each case. The team that runs them in all three places ends up with something most teams never have — a flow whose start, middle, and end are honestly described.

The fix

The fix from this exercise has three parts and the team can do them in fifteen minutes once the gap is visible.

First, write down the team's definition of done. The actual one, the one the team will stand behind. Not aspirational — what the team will genuinely refuse to move a card past until it is true. This list is short. Three to six items. Things like "merged", "tested by someone who is not the author", "behind no feature flag", "running in the environment the customer uses." The list is the team's, not yours.

Second, draw the post-done steps on the board. Even if those steps are not the team's work — the stakeholder verification, the marketing sign-off, the deployment window — they exist, they have a person, and they have a time. Put them on the board with the name of the person responsible. The first time this is done, half the items have nobody's name on them, and that is the next finding: nobody owned them, which is why they have been taking weeks.

Third, write the definition of ready the same way. A short list of what has to be true before a card is allowed into "in progress." Not "fully understood" — that is aspirational. Something concrete: "acceptance criteria the team agrees on", "no open external dependency the team cannot resolve themselves", "the question that obviously needs answering has been answered." Three to six items here, too.

Do not let the team write the long version of either list. A definition of done with thirty items is the same kind of dishonest as a board with fourteen columns — it implies a precision the team will not actually hold, and the first time it is inconvenient it will be ignored, and the next time too, and after that the list does not exist any more.

When the gates are clear

It happens, more often with definition-of-done than with the previous two exercises, that the team already has a clear and honest definition.

Sometimes that definition is small — "merged and tested" — and the team works in a place where "done" really does mean the customer has it the next day. Sometimes it is larger and the team has already drawn the post-done steps on the board because they have done this work before. When that is the case, do the walk-through anyway, just on one card, to verify the definition matches what actually happens. If it does, the team passes. Say so and move on.

The principle from chapter 12 holds: the right amount of definition is the amount the team needs to hold its agreements, not the amount that fills out a coaching template. A team that already runs an honest definition does not need a longer one.

When done is light

I worked with a team once that was productive in every way the board could measure. Stories moved into "done" reliably, every sprint. Reviews were thorough, testing was complete, acceptance criteria were met. The definition of done was light — reviews and testing done, acceptance criteria met — and the team hit it every sprint.

The problem was that nothing in "done" was actually in production. Moving anything in front of a customer required the product owner to give the go-ahead, and the product owner could rarely give it. Sometimes it was because a customer needed to be trained on the new feature first, or comms had to go out before release. Sometimes it was because she was on holiday. Most often it was simply because her day job did not leave her enough time with us to make the call. The card sat in "done" and aged.

The pile of things waiting for better days grew. Who should be trained on this feature now that it had changed? How was the team supposed to work around this constraint in the system while the fix waited for resourcing? Unanswered questions sat in production, untested by anyone outside the team, undiscovered until the software was eventually used in anger by a real customer. By the time those bugs surfaced — weeks later, sometimes months — the knowledge the team had built up about the feature was already legacy. Half the team had moved onto other work. The mental model that had built the thing had been swapped out by then for the mental model of whatever was current.

The board kept telling the team — and anyone reading the board, anyone reporting up from the board — that the work was done. The customers experienced none of it. The team's velocity was excellent and its actual impact was almost zero, and nobody could see that from the board because the board did not show what happened past "done."

This was the team's definition of done at work, and it was a lie of omission. It was not the wrong definition for the work the team controlled. It was the wrong place to put the finish line. The finish line was somewhere past the product owner's queue, and the queue was on holiday.

The line they could not hold

I worked with another team that had the opposite problem — its work blocked the moment it entered progress. Sprints were planned full of stories, the team picked up the first one on day one, and within a day or two it was sitting in "blocked." Then the second story. Then the third. By the middle of the sprint the team was running around the board chasing whatever had moved one step because a customer had finally answered an email.

The team got excited about the DoR exercise. They saw it as a way to finally push back on the product manager, who had a habit of dropping half-formed work into the sprint backlog — work that depended on a customer giving the team access to their infrastructure for a final deploy and test. We ran the session. The product manager listened politely, and at the end he gave us the line product managers give when something is real: "this is all very obvious."

A few days later we planned a sprint. I asked, story by story, whether each one met the DoR we had just agreed on. They mostly did, except for the ones that needed client bookings. The product manager said he could not do any better. He could not control the clients.

The sprint started. The first story blocked on day one. We walked the board every day, painfully. I dug into the question of why client engagement was always late, and asked the team to talk to the sales team and work out something better. No volunteers. Just *we can't, we can't. What if we can?* I asked back, with enough edge that the room felt it, and made them imagine, for a moment, what the board would look like if this one thing were fixed. Then I voluntold a senior developer to take the conversation to sales and get the customer bookings tied to the planning cycle.

It did not work. Or rather, the conversation happened and nothing changed. The team kept picking up cards that did not meet the DoR they had themselves written, because the alternative was an empty sprint, and an empty sprint was a thing nobody in the team was willing to defend. Every week the same thing. Cards blocked. The "blocked" column grew. Sometimes the team would all scramble to one card when a customer finally responded and the card would move one step, then stop again. There was no predictability and no flow.

Most of the time, when a team runs the DoR exercise, the team finally has the line they needed and they hold it. Sometimes — and this team is the case — the team can see the right line clearly, can write it down, and still cannot bring itself to defend it when the next sprint starts. The exercise found the problem. The team did not act on it. The dysfunction continued, and the board kept telling the lie the team had already named.

Three ways it goes wrong

The first is that the team writes a definition of done so long and so cautious it becomes a wishlist nothing satisfies. A definition of done that genuinely cannot be met for an ordinary story is one the team will quietly ignore, which is worse than not having one. Three to six things. Each one a thing the team will actually refuse to move a card past until it is true.

The second is that the post-done steps get drawn on the board with nobody's name attached. The point of drawing them is not the picture; it is to surface the fact that they have no owner. A step on the board with no owner is a queue with no end. If the team cannot name the owner of a step, that is the first thing to fix — not the step's time, the step's name.

The third is that the team tries to make customer-done the team's done. Sometimes this works. Often it does not, because the things between team-done and customer-done are genuinely outside the team's control. Trying to own them inside the team produces frustration and missed sprints. The honest move is to draw them, name the owner, and treat the wait as a flow problem the team can surface but not always close. That sometimes means going up the chain to ask why the owner is not closing it — which is its own conversation, and the next chapter is where some of those conversations end.

The rescue

If you suspect your team's "done" is a lie — and if your team ever talks about a story being "done but not deployed", or "done but waiting on the PO", or "done but blocked on legal", it is — you do not need a workshop. You need one card, fifteen minutes, and the team.

Pick a card the team called done last sprint. Walk through what has happened to it since. List every step. Look at the list. Decide what done has to mean to be a thing the team can honestly commit to, write that down, and draw the rest of the steps on the board with the names of the people who owe them. By the end of the fifteen minutes the team will know two things it did not know at the start: how long the work past done has actually been taking, and who has been quietly carrying it.

The bigger thing the team will eventually know is that some of the post-done steps were never going to happen at all. Decisions that had no owner. Sign-offs that lapsed silently. Deployments deferred until they could no longer be done at all. That is the next chapter.

Chapter 15: Where Ideas Come to Die

THE hardest decision any team makes is to stop something.

A team that has run the exercises in this part of the book has just learned to see decision debt in three places. Hidden inside its columns. Sitting in its column times. Past the end of its board. What it has not yet learned to see is the largest pile of all — the decisions the team has been quietly avoiding for so long that they have stopped looking like decisions. The initiative that started two years ago, has cost six engineer-years so far, and is now demonstrably worse than what it was meant to replace. The recurring meeting that lost its point three reorganisations ago and is still on the calendar. The backlog of four hundred tickets nobody is going to refine. The "blocker" column that holds work everyone agrees should not still be in flight but somehow is.

These are not decision queues. They are graveyards.

The difference matters. A queue is decisions waiting to be made. A graveyard is decisions the team has stopped pretending to make at all. Queues get drained when somebody picks up a card. Graveyards have to be cleared, and the team has to be the one to do it, because the act of clearing them is the act of admitting that something the team was doing was not worth continuing.

This is the chapter Part 3 has been building toward, and it is the most uncomfortable chapter in the part. The exercises so far have been about making invisible work visible. This one is about looking at what becomes visible and deciding to kill some of it.

The exercise

Pick a list. Any list — the active initiatives, the recurring meetings on the team calendar, the standing processes, the items in the backlog older than three months. Run the question down the list, item by item: *if we were not already doing this, would we start it today?*

That is the exercise. One question, one list. It takes as long as the list is long.

Every item that gets a no is a candidate for the graveyard. Not for the next planning session, not for "we should discuss this in the retro" — for the graveyard. You write down what gets killed. You do it now. Tomorrow the same items will still get a no, and the day after, and the team will go on paying for them until somebody says stop.

The rest of this chapter is about why that single question is the most expensive thing on the page for most teams to actually answer honestly, and what it takes to act on the answers.

Why "stop" is the hardest decision

A team that runs the cycle-time exercise from chapter 13 and finds a column with a huge gap will, more often than not, attack it. The fix is concrete. The team can see what done looks like.

The decision is *do something*, and doing something is what teams are built to do.

The decision the graveyard exercise asks for is the opposite. It is *do nothing — and tell the people who have been counting on this that you are no longer going to do it.* That is a structurally different kind of move. Doing something has a roadmap and a team-channel announcement and a small win at the end of a sprint. Not doing something has none of those. It has a hard conversation, and it has the absence of an outcome where there used to be motion, and the only evidence it was the right call is the time the team gets back.

That asymmetry is why graveyards form. The team can clearly see that the migration is failing, that the meeting has not produced a decision in months, that the initiative was funded for reasons that no longer apply — and still, week by week, choose to continue, because continuing is easier than stopping. Each individual week the cost of continuing is small. The cumulative cost is enormous, and it never gets paid except in the quiet way of nothing ever shipping.

Decision debt becomes a graveyard exactly when the team has lost the habit of making "stop" decisions. The fix is not better prioritisation. It is the team relearning that stop is a decision, and the cost of not making it is real.

The texture of a software graveyard

The reason this is not a generic "sunk cost fallacy" chapter is that every business book in the world has already told you about sunk cost. What it has not told you is what sunk cost looks like in software delivery, and what it looks like is specific and ugly.

The half-built feature whose original requester left the company a year ago, but the feature is still in flight and nobody will euthanise it because three engineers have spent a year on it.

The framework migration that is sixty percent done and already worse than what it is replacing — the new version is missing capabilities the old one had, the team is maintaining both in parallel, and the path to "done" is now genuinely longer than rolling back to the original.

The platform initiative that was greenlit when there were three teams who would use it, and is now being built for the one team that has not migrated away yet.

The "north star" architecture that was set during the last reorganisation, has been overtaken by two more reorganisations since, and has never been formally retired, so it is still cited in design reviews and still consulted in planning, and still wrong.

The compliance process that was added after an incident in 2019, no longer addresses anything the company is genuinely at risk for, and adds a week to every release.

None of these are sunk cost in the textbook sense. They are sunk cost dressed in the specific clothes software delivery wears, and naming them out loud is most of the work this chapter is here to do. A team that recognises one of these in its own work has done more than half of the kill.

The tickets you had the sense never to create

There is a smaller version of this exercise that you can run on the spot, every day, without a session. It is worth its own name because it stops the graveyard from forming in the first place.

A tester finds an edge case. The business analyst and product manager, looking at the edge case, tell her to ignore it. The tester comes to you and asks whether she should pass the work back to the developer and raise a new ticket for the missing feature. The question you ask is not "should you pass it back" and not "should you raise a ticket." The question is: *what is the best use of your time today to get this thing done and into the customer's hands as quickly as possible?*

The tester thinks. Decides the edge case is not worth a hand-back. Moves on.

That is a ticket you just did not create. A small decision that, scaled across a year and a team, is the difference between a backlog that is alive and a graveyard. The graveyard is not only the place dead tickets go — it is also the tickets a healthier team would have had the sense never to create. Every "we should track this" that gets converted into a card is a future decision the team is committing to make, and most teams accumulate those commitments faster than they retire them.

Stopping the graveyard from forming is cheaper than clearing it later. The question — *what is the best use of your time today to get this into the customer's hands?* — is the smallest, most useful version of the larger question this chapter exists for. It costs nothing and it works.

Ask, don't tell — and the cost of asking

The same facilitation ladder from chapter 12 runs here, but the room behaves differently than it did before, and the ladder has to be adapted.

The first rung is still to ask. *If we were not already doing this, would we start it today?* The question is enough. The team will know which items get a no. The hard part is not finding them — it is what happens after.

The second rung, if the team is reluctant to answer honestly, is not an anecdote. It is to ask the inverse — the question that is harder to evade. *Knowing what we know now, would the original sponsor of this initiative ask for it again?* Almost nobody, when asked that question on a specific item, says yes for something the rest of the room has already silently doubted.

The third rung is not show-and-tell. There is no card to walk through, because the items are visible already. The third rung is to ask, plainly: *what would it cost us to stop this, and what would it cost us to continue?* Where the second number is larger than the first, you have a candidate for the graveyard, and the team has just done the arithmetic in front of itself.

The cost of asking these questions, unlike the others in this part, is that some of the answers will produce conflict outside the room. The person who started the initiative two years ago may still be in the company, may still be senior, and may still believe in it. The recurring meeting may belong to a manager who put it on the calendar and likes that it is there. The compliance process may exist because somebody promised the regulator it would. None of these are reasons to leave the items on the list. They are reasons to do the work of taking them off — and that work is political, not technical.

This is the place where the delivery manager's job stops being about facilitating the team and starts being about spending capital outside it. The graveyard cannot be cleared without somebody upstairs being told that things they cared about are no longer being done. The cheap fix at the team level is expensive at the org level. That is not a reason to skip it. It is the part of the work that earns the title on the door.

The fix

The fix from the graveyard exercise has three moves and the team can do the first two in the room.

First, write down what is being killed. Each item, with one sentence saying why. No grand explanation. No internal political language. The shortest honest version: *this is not worth what it is costing.* If the team cannot say that sentence about an item, that item is not a candidate yet — leave it on the list and come back when the team can.

Second, decide who has to be told. For each killed item, somebody outside the room is affected. The original requester, the manager who cared, the stakeholder whose name was on the brief. Write that down too. The act of writing it is what makes the kill real. A graveyard exercise that ends with "we will stop doing it" but no list of people to inform is an exercise that has produced a feeling, not a decision.

Third — and this one is the delivery manager's, not the team's — go and have the conversations. This is where the political cost lands. The conversations are not bad. They are usually shorter than people fear, because the other side often half-knew the item was dying. But they have to happen, and they have to be specific. *We are no longer doing X, because Y, and the reason I am telling you is Z.* Then you live with the answer, which is sometimes a fight, sometimes a relief, and sometimes a no — in which case you keep the advice on record and watch.

The kill is real when the work stops, the people who needed to know have been told, and the team has the time back. Until all three are true, the item is in limbo — which is worse than either continuing it honestly or killing it cleanly.

When the graveyard is empty

Sometimes you run this exercise and find no graveyard. Every active initiative still has its purpose. Every meeting still has its job. The standing processes still address risks that are still real. The backlog has been pruned recently. The team has been clearing as it goes.

When that happens, the exercise has done what every other exercise in this part does at its honest end: it has told you the dysfunction is not here. Say so. Move on. A team that has not let a graveyard accumulate is, in this book's terms, doing the most disciplined version of the work. Tell them so, and look elsewhere.

The honest version of this finding is rarer than the others, because graveyards are sticky in a way long columns and unclear definitions are not. But it does happen. When it does, the move is the one this book has been recommending throughout: recognise it, leave it alone, and find the room where there is actually something to fix.

The project you cannot kill

The version of the graveyard exercise the rest of this chapter describes is the version where the kill is available to you — where you can run the question, write down the no's, and act on them. There is another case, and it is more common than the book would like to admit. The project that is most clearly dead is sometimes the one you have no authority over. Your job in that case is not to facilitate a kill. It is to give honest advice, put it on record, keep giving it, and not let the project absorb the team's belief in its own work while you wait for somebody upstairs to make the call.

What that looks like in practice.

I once worked at a long-standing business — the kind whose name the reader would recognise — that had hired us to rebuild a legacy system it had been running for around twenty years. There was a support engineer on staff who had been with that system the whole time. Twenty years of his job had been maintaining it, documenting it, building a private body of knowledge about what was broken in it and what he thought the fixes should be. When the rebuild started and the team began to actually move work, he kept asking us to fix low-priority bugs he had been carrying in his head for years. Each one was small. Each one pulled the team off the main line.

The first time a colleague asked me, with the smallest chuckle, whether I had "been through the support guy's presentation" yet, I did not understand the question. I understood it about a fortnight later when, on a Friday at three in the afternoon — the moment of the week when no one has the energy to refuse anything — the support engineer asked me whether I had a minute. The minute took an hour, and the hour was a sixty-four-page presentation backed by several Excel spreadsheets, covering every fix he had ever envisioned and every feature he thought the system should grow.

The honest advice, after the meeting, was that the software was not worth saving. The business case for the rebuild did not stack up. The right move was to bin it and buy something off the shelf. I said so, on record, and was ignored. The rebuild continued. The support engineer kept feeding bugs into the backlog. The presentation made more rounds. The team kept doing the work because the work had been bought and paid for, and the call to stop was not theirs to make.

Eventually — months later than it should have been — the business reached the same conclusion. They bought an off-the-shelf product, retired the legacy system, and binned the rebuild. The support engineer lost the pet project he had spent two decades on. The team got their lives back and moved onto more meaningful work. The system, finally, went somewhere it could not consume any more of the company's time.

That story is not a victory lap. The graveyard was real, the advice was correct, and the kill happened — but not because the delivery manager facilitated it. It happened because the business above the team eventually noticed what the delivery manager had been saying. My job in those months had been to give honest advice and to keep the team from letting the doomed project drain their belief in their own work. That is the version of this exercise you sometimes have to settle for, and recognising when you are in it is part of the work.

Three ways it goes wrong

The first is that the team kills the easy ones and leaves the expensive ones. Two recurring meetings get axed; the multi-quarter initiative everybody knows is dying stays alive because the politics are too hard. The exercise has then produced a feeling of progress without the actual return. The test for the exercise is the size of what is killed, not the count. One large item retired beats six small ones cancelled.

The second is that the kill is announced but the work continues. The team says “we are no longer doing X” in the room and then continues doing X next sprint, because some piece of it was attached to something else and never got unwound. The kill has to be real in the next sprint’s planning, or the graveyard quietly absorbs the announcement and goes on.

The third is treating the exercise as a one-off event rather than a habit. Graveyards form continuously. A team that runs this exercise once and feels finished has, six months later, a new graveyard. The exercise is most valuable as a rhythm — once a quarter, on a low-stakes Friday, you ask the question across the lists and you cull. It works the way pruning a garden works: small, regular, indispensable.

The rescue

If you suspect your team is carrying a graveyard — and if anyone on the team has, in the last month, made the joke about a meeting or an initiative that nobody can cancel, you are — you do not need a restructure. You need one list and one question.

Pick the smallest list first. The recurring meetings. Run the question down it. Mark every no. Then run the same question, the same afternoon, on the next-smallest list — the standing processes, or the items in the backlog older than a quarter. Then on the largest — the active initiatives. By the time you have run the question across all four lists, you will have a graveyard’s worth of items written down. The work is not running the question. The work is killing what the question revealed.

Do one thing this week. The smallest one. Cancel one meeting that has not produced a decision in months. Tell the people who were on the invitation. Get the time back. Watch the team's reaction. The graveyard you are clearing is also the thing that has been telling the team, week by week, that decisions are permanent and have to be lived with. Clearing it teaches the team the opposite — that stopping is as much a decision as starting. A team that knows how to stop is a team ready for what comes next.

Chapter 16: The People Who Can Stop You

STAKEHOLDER engagement comes down to one line: keep the relevant people in the loop. Almost everything else is detail.

Most of what gets called a "stakeholder problem" is not a stakeholder being difficult. It is a stakeholder who has been left out of a loop they needed to be in, reacting the way anyone reacts when they discover something important happened without them. People are not, by and large, trying to derail your work. They want to be involved, or they want to be informed — regularly, and whenever something changes. Give them that and most of the friction you were bracing for never arrives.

This matters more than it looks, because stakeholders are where direction and scope decisions actually live. The team can run perfect ceremonies and still stall, because a decision it depends on is sitting unmade in a stakeholder's head, or a stakeholder who was never brought along vetoes the work late, when reversing it is most expensive. An uninformed stakeholder is decision debt in human form — a decision the team needs, stuck outside the team. Keeping people in the loop is how you keep those decisions moving.

Map the stakeholders first

One of the first things to do on any new engagement is map the stakeholders. Not elaborately — a simple map with the data points that actually matter.

A full RACI — responsible, accountable, consulted, informed, mapped across every task — is the textbook tool, and it is usually overcomplicated for initial purposes. What you actually need to know at the start is smaller: who do you go to in what situation, who needs to be kept in the loop, and how often. That is most of it. Who decides scope. Who decides go-live. Who can unblock a dependency. Who will be upset if they hear about a change secondhand. Write those down and you have a working map.

The piece people skip is oversight. When you are building software, you need to know not just who the decision-makers are but what kind of oversight they want — how closely they want to watch, in what form, at what cadence. Some stakeholders want a weekly summary and otherwise to be left alone. Some want to be in the room for every significant call. Getting this wrong in either direction causes friction: under-inform the close-watcher and they feel blindsided; over-inform the hands-off sponsor and you have become noise they tune out. Ask each key stakeholder, early, how they want to be kept across the work. Then do that.

Establishing how the team's work gets reported — upward to leadership, sideways to peer teams and dependencies — is one of the first moves of an engagement, not something you figure out after the first thing goes wrong.

Give them what they need; tell them what you need

The highest-leverage stakeholder activity is also the most overlooked: giving stakeholders what they need to do their own jobs and endorse your work.

Every stakeholder has someone they answer to and something they are accountable for. If providing a stakeholder with a clear progress summary lets them reassure their own boss and keep backing your team, that summary is not administrative overhead — it is one of the biggest bottleneck-removing activities available to you. A stakeholder who can confidently endorse your work upward clears a path. A stakeholder who can't, because you never gave them what they needed to, becomes a blocker, often without meaning to.

The same runs in reverse, and teams forget this half constantly. Make stakeholders aware of what you need from them — the decision you're waiting on, the access you don't have, the sign-off that's holding up a release. And make them aware of what success requires of them, not just of the team. Stakeholder engagement is not the team performing for an audience. It is a two-way arrangement where each side tells the other what it needs to keep the work moving. The team that only ever reports outward, and never states its own needs clearly, ends up blocked by decisions it never explicitly asked anyone to make.

Communicate the plan, the progress, and the constraints

A team almost always has to do two things for its stakeholders: communicate a plan, and show progress against it. Both are necessary. Both are where teams quietly set themselves up to fail, by communicating the plan and the progress while staying silent about the constraints.

The constraint that matters most early is uncertainty itself. When you take over a team, you don't yet know how it works — how fast it really moves, where it gets stuck, what its actual capacity is. Any timeline or roadmap you produce in that period is a guess dressed as a forecast, and it has to be communicated as such. "Here is our current plan, and here is why it should be taken with a grain of salt until we have a few sprints of real data" is not weakness. It is the thing that stops a rough early estimate from hardening into a commitment you'll be held to later. Stakeholders can handle uncertainty when you name it. What they can't forgive is confident precision that turns out to be fiction.

Which brings us to the most beloved instrument of false precision in the business.

The Gantt chart

People still love Gantt charts. I don't have anything against them — they have their place. But there are a few things worth acknowledging honestly.

For technology projects, try to count on one hand the number of times you've seen a Gantt chart turn out accurate. They are works of fiction. They get reworked, over and over, until the line between fairy tale and true story blurs enough that the chart is finally ready to show the most senior stakeholders. I have never enjoyed preparing one with mid-level execs and then being asked to prove it will come true, because for software it mostly won't.

A Gantt chart is a lens on a project at a single point in time, showing the thinking at that point in time. For predictable industries — where the work is well understood and rarely surprises anyone — they are reasonably accurate and don't change much. For software engineering, where the work is discovery as much as construction, a Gantt is accurate for one instant and starts decaying immediately. Using one to model a software timeline precisely is like wearing welding goggles instead of sunglasses to block out the sun. Sure, both block the sun. But do you really want to wander around in welding goggles?

None of this means refuse to produce them. Execs often genuinely need a Gantt — it is the format their world runs on, the thing they report upward with. The move is not to refuse the chart. It is to provide it and make the limitations explicit, every time: this is our best current picture, it will change as we learn, and the further out it projects the less you should trust it. Hand over the chart and the caveat together, permanently bolted to each other. A Gantt delivered without its limitations stated is a promise you didn't mean to make.

Workshops, and the cost of skipping them

When you're setting up a project or an engagement, a workshop is one of the best ways to get every stakeholder onto the same page — about what's being built, in what order, and how progress and issues will be communicated. The output you want is consensus: a shared list of what matters, agreed by the people who'll later be asked to live with it. Run one well and you've pre-empted most of the friction that would otherwise surface later as objections.

One practical detail makes workshops work: a parking lot. When someone raises something real but off-topic, or important but not for now, it goes on the parking lot — visibly captured, to be revisited — rather than either derailing the session or being waved away. People will tolerate not resolving their issue today. They will not tolerate feeling unheard. The parking lot is how everyone leaves feeling their concern was registered, even the ones whose concerns you didn't get to.

I learned the cost of skipping the workshop by cleaning up after someone who did. A client once brought in a third-party expert to produce a plan for fixing some specific problems. He consulted one or two managers in the area, went away, and came back with a polished presentation full of highly opinionated recommendations. They were never going to fly — and worse, the stakeholders he hadn't bothered to involve caught wind of what was happening and shut the whole thing down, on the entirely reasonable grounds that nobody had been consulted and the recommendations were unrealistic. The expertise might even have been sound. It didn't matter. Recommendations nobody had input into were recommendations nobody would own.

I was brought in to do what should have been done at the start: run workshops with all the stakeholders. We began by establishing roles and operating protocols — who wanted to be kept in the loop on what, and when. Then we walked through every problem that existed and sized each by complexity and impact (the same matrix from the diagnosis chapters — that prioritisation logic works on problems as well as on fixes). By the end we had a list of what we'd tackle first, with full consensus across the board. The work that followed stuck, not because the plan was smarter than the expert's, but because the people who had to back it had built it.

When a stakeholder is the blocker

Keeping people in the loop assumes the people want the work to succeed. Usually that holds. Occasionally it does not, and the hardest stakeholder situation you'll face is the one where a stakeholder is quietly working against you while appearing to cooperate.

I once inherited a team that could not get anything finished. The pattern looked like ordinary churn: the business analyst would meet the stakeholders, agree the functionality, get the requirements approved, and the team would build. Then at go-live the demo would surface edge cases and missing functionality, the stakeholders would object, and the cycle would restart. A fail loop with no exit. I was brought in to find the problem and get the thing into production.

I started, as always, with one-on-ones. One was unusually enlightening. A team member mentioned — in confidence, and nervous about it — that they'd heard from someone on the stakeholder side that the senior stakeholder driving the project had wanted, all along, to buy an off-the-shelf product rather than build one. Suddenly the fail loop made sense. The endless edge cases weren't a quality problem. The stakeholders didn't mind burning the team's time, because every failed go-live was evidence for the case the stakeholder actually wanted to make: that building this in-house was a mistake.

I couldn't reveal the source, and I couldn't accuse anyone of anything I'd heard secondhand in confidence. What I could do was change the structure so the stakeholder had to commit instead of stall. The fail loop worked for him precisely because nothing was ever final — there was always another round, another edge case, more of the team's time to burn. So I removed the ability to stall. I had the team run sessions themed as "final requirements before we launch into production," and I told the senior stakeholders we'd completed the final round and were getting formal sign-off as the last gate before the first production launch — with the understanding that anything we discovered afterward could be remedied tactically once live, which internal apps allow.

The stakeholder signed off. About a day later the entire project was put on hold, and shortly after, axed. Forcing a real decision — making the stakes high and the moment unavoidable — had pushed him into the open. He couldn't keep the loop running once the next step was a launch he didn't actually want, so the real position finally surfaced. And the project landing in the bin was the right outcome. Building an off-the-shelf product inside an unsuitable low-code codebase, by five people typing it out by hand, never made business sense. The decision to kill it had been owed for months. All the sign-off gate did was collapse the decision debt that the fail loop had been hiding.

Two things generalise from that. First, when a team is stuck in a loop that never converges no matter how much it delivers, consider that the blocker might not be the work — it might be a stakeholder for whom the work failing is the preferred outcome. Second, the way you handle that is not accusation, which you usually can't support and which burns the source who told you. It is to remove the conditions that let the stalling continue: force the decision into a moment where the stakeholder has to commit or visibly refuse. The hidden agenda cannot survive being made to choose.

Failure modes

Reporting outward, never stating needs. The team diligently sends updates upward and never tells stakeholders what it needs from them. Decisions the team depends on sit unmade because nobody was explicitly asked. The fix is symmetry: every progress report also names what the team is waiting on and from whom.

The Gantt without the caveat. A timeline gets handed to senior stakeholders as if it were a commitment, the caveats lost somewhere on the way up. When it slips — and for software it will — the team is held to a promise it never meant to make. The fix is to bolt the limitations to the chart permanently, and to restate them every time it travels upward.

The stakeholder who was left out. Someone with real influence wasn't in the loop, finds out late, and shuts things down —

not always because the work is wrong, but because they weren't consulted. The third-party expert's whole engagement died this way. The fix is the stakeholder map and the early workshop: identify everyone whose endorsement you'll eventually need, and bring them in before there's something to object to, not after.

The loop that never converges. Every milestone surfaces new objections, the work never ships, and more rounds always follow. Sometimes genuine discovery; sometimes, when it goes on too long, a stakeholder for whom failure is the goal. The fix for the benign version is tighter scope and a real definition of done. The fix for the other version is to force the decision into the open, as above.

The rescue, in week one

On a new engagement, map the stakeholders before you touch the work. Who decides what, who needs to be kept in the loop, how often, and what kind of oversight each one wants. Half an hour with a notepad and a few quick conversations gets you most of it.

Then set up the loops. Agree with each key stakeholder how they want to be kept across the work, and start doing it from the first week — before there's a problem to report, so that the channel exists and is trusted by the time you need it for bad news. If the engagement is big enough or contested enough, run a workshop early: get everyone in a room, establish who's informed of what and when, size the problems together, and leave with a consensus list. Use a parking lot so nobody leaves feeling unheard.

And communicate your constraints from the start — especially that your early timelines are estimates made before you understand the team, to be firmed up as real data arrives. Naming that uncertainty up front is what stops it being used against you later.

The signal the rescue has taken: stakeholders stop being surprised. No late vetoes, no blindsided executive, no expert-style ambush from someone who was left out. The decisions the team depends on get made when the team needs them, because the people who make them have been in the loop all along.

Part Four: When the Bottleneck Is the Whole Job

For three parts now this book has argued one thing. Most of what slows your delivery is not the work. It is decisions waiting to be made. Decisions stuck in columns the board does not show. Decisions queued behind one overloaded person. Decisions sitting past the end of "done" because nobody owns the next step. Decisions accumulated into a graveyard nobody will clear. Three parts of cheap fixes attacking decision debt in each of the places it gathers.

If you have run those fixes — or even read them honestly — you have probably already done the arithmetic in your head. Most of your team's cycle time, in most weeks, is not code being written. It is people, calendars, gates, and waiting. The code was never the long part.

This is the part where I have to admit how this book started. The original case for writing it was a quieter version of the one you have just read. Decision latency mattered, but everybody on the team was busy and the code was hard, and the chapters of Part 3 were nice-to-haves rather than emergencies. A team that fixed its hidden columns saved days. A team that did not fix them shipped anyway, eventually, because the engineering still took weeks and the wait took a fraction.

Then the engineering started taking hours.

Not all of it. Not always. But for more and more of the work — the boilerplate, the tests, the first pass at almost any feature, the routine refactor — what used to take an engineer most of a week now takes a competent engineer with the right tooling most of an afternoon.

That changes the ratio.

When the code took weeks, a manager sitting on a decision for three days was annoying. The team had plenty of code in flight to keep moving, and the three-day wait was a sliver of the sprint. When the code takes hours, three days of decision-wait is the entire timeline of the work. The team finishes whatever it had, looks up, and discovers there is nothing in the queue ready to be picked up — because all the things in the queue are waiting on a decision somewhere, and decisions have not got any faster.

That is the shift this part is about. AI did not change the bottleneck. The bottleneck was always decision debt. What AI changed is the cost of decision debt, and the cost has gone from annoying to everything. A team carrying the same amount of decision debt it had three years ago is now spending the majority of its cycle time on the consequences of that debt, because the rest of its cycle time has compressed to almost nothing.

There is a second-order version of this that almost nobody has acted on. If AI has genuinely compressed the build, then build is no longer where the team's capacity should be concentrated — and yet most teams are still shaped exactly as they were when build was the long pole. Same ratio of people to roles, same shape, organised around a bottleneck that has moved. Most organisations rolled AI out as though it were a faster development environment — a tool the existing team uses to do the existing work more quickly. That misses the point entirely. AI did not make the team faster at its old job; it changed which job is the constraint. A team optimised for a constraint that no longer exists is, by definition, the wrong shape for the work in front of it.

The question this forces is uncomfortable, and most teams have not asked it: if the work has moved, why hasn't the team? A group built around three people writing code may now need its weight somewhere else entirely — more capacity to verify that the faster-produced code is actually right, or more capacity upstream, where the decisions that feed the work are made. Which one depends on where your constraint actually landed, and the only way to know is to look. The mistake is not picking the wrong answer. The mistake is not re-asking the question at all — leaving the team in the shape it took when code was the thing that was scarce.

There is a way of saying this that the book is going to keep clear of, and you have probably already read versions of it elsewhere. The wrong frame is "AI is making delivery harder," or "AI is exposing weaknesses we never had to worry about before," or any variation that treats AI as a complication of an older, simpler world. The simpler world was not simpler. It was the same world, with decision debt growing quietly while engineering soaked up the visible time. AI did not produce a new problem. It exposed an old one — the same one Parts 1, 2, and 3 of this book have been talking about — by making it impossible to keep ignoring.

What that means in practice is a discipline the previous parts implied but did not name. Teams used to be able to let decision debt accumulate quietly and pay it down occasionally, when a particular column had got bad enough to notice. That economy is over. The cost has risen enough that minimising decision debt has to become deliberate, ongoing work — naming it the moment it starts to form, in standups, in planning, in the corridor — and not just an exercise the team runs when something breaks. The mindset that comes with this part is that the team is now in the business of attending to decision debt the way it has always been in the business of attending to code quality. Not constantly, not anxiously, but as a standing part of how it works.

That is the frame for this part. The chapters that follow take each of the locations where decision debt accumulates — at the front of the work, past the team-done line, in the queue of unmade decisions above the team, in the product roadmap that feeds the queue — and ask the same question. What does this look like when the code has compressed and the decisions have not? Which gates need to be settled before the work starts, rather than figured out while it runs? Which handoffs need to disappear, because there is no longer enough work-time on either side of them to absorb the wait?

The fixes in this part are still cheap in the sense the rest of the book has used the word. They cost decisions, conversations, and changes to ways of working, not money. But they are not as optional as they were a year ago. The teams who carried decision debt in 2022 paid for it in slow sprints. The teams who carry decision debt now pay for it in being unable to ship at all on weeks when their tooling has handed them a sprint's worth of code by Tuesday.

This is also the part of the book where the lesson of the first three parts becomes most concrete. A team that has done the work of Parts 1 through 3 — that has run the exercises, mapped its real flow, killed its graveyard, and learned to subtract — is the team that absorbs this shift cleanly. A team that has not done that work is the team that finds itself busier than ever, with less to show for it, blaming the tooling for a problem the tooling only revealed.

The bottleneck has become the whole job. The good news, if you have read this far, is that the bottleneck was the only thing this book ever pointed at.

Chapter 17: Ready Has To Mean More Than It Did

WHEN a build takes hours instead of days, there is no longer enough build-time to absorb an unresolved question.

The old way of working ran on a hidden subsidy. The slow part — the building — quietly bought time for the fast questions to get answered. A card could be pulled into progress with a fuzzy edge or two, and by the time the developer reached them, someone had worked the answer out. Building was slow enough to hide the deciding inside it. That economy is over. Now the card is "done" by Tuesday, and the team isn't sure whether what it built was what anyone wanted — because the question of what was wanted was supposed to get resolved later in the week, and later in the week is now after the build is finished.

When the building stops absorbing the team's unmade decisions, those decisions have to be made before the build starts. Which means the front gate of the board — the definition of ready — has to carry weight it never had to carry before.

What "ready" used to mean, and what it has to mean

What "ready" used to mean was, roughly, *the team can start.* The card has acceptance criteria. The dependencies are identified. The product owner is reachable. Anything not yet settled can be settled as the work runs. That was a perfectly honest definition for a world where the work ran for days.

What "ready" has to mean now is closer to *the team can finish.* Every decision the team is going to need during the build must already have either an answer or an owner-and-a-deadline, because there is no longer enough run-time in the build to chase a decision in flight. A card whose acceptance criteria are clear but whose definition of "good enough to ship" is fuzzy is not ready. A card whose dependencies are identified but whose blocker on a stakeholder is not chased is not ready. A card whose test plan is "QA will figure out how to test it" is not ready, because by the time QA has figured it out the build is done and waiting.

This is the change of definition the part is about. The bar has moved from "we know enough to start" to "we know enough to land." If you use the old bar in the new ratio, you will get exactly what teams using AI tooling without doing this work are reporting now: faster output, more rework, and the work no closer to being done in any meaningful sense.

What has to be in the new definition

In practice there are three additions to the definition the team probably already has, and they are the same three additions for almost every team I have walked through this.

The first is *what does good look like, in terms specific enough that two different team members would build the same thing from them.* Not a paragraph of intent. Not "make it match the design." The actual operating definition. If the work is to add a feature, what is the user-visible behaviour, and what is explicitly out of scope? If the work is to fix a bug, what is the test case the fix has to pass? If the work is to refactor, what is the observable behaviour the refactor must preserve? In the old ratio you could discover the answers to these as the work ran; in the new one you have to write them down before the work starts, because the work will be over before the discovery has finished.

The product owners doing this well are using AI tooling for exactly the same reason their teams are — to produce the artefact faster. A working wireframe, an interactive sketch, a short prototype of the intended behaviour, generated in the time it used to take to write a requirements document. The artefact disambiguates better than prose ever could, and producing it is no longer the expensive part of the work.

The second is *how the team will know it got it.* The test plan. Not the test cases — those are the team's job. But the level the test plan has to reach before the work starts. Is automated regression enough? Is there a specific user journey that has to pass? Does someone need to look at it in production behind a flag? This used to be implicit, because manual testing at the end of the build would catch most of it and the build was long enough to absorb the manual pass. Now the manual pass is the bottleneck, and the test plan has to be settled in advance so the testing capacity the team has is spent on the things that genuinely need it, not on figuring out what to test.

The third is *what decisions the team is going to need, and from whom.* Not a hope that the product owner will be reachable. The actual list. For every decision the team can foresee — and the team can foresee most of them, if asked at the right moment — write the question, the owner, and the date by which the answer is needed. If the question is "will the customer accept a feature flag for the first release", the owner is the product owner, and the date is the third day of the sprint, then either the product owner answers it before the work starts or the answer becomes a known risk on the card. What you do not do is pull the card hoping the question will not come up, because it will, and you no longer have weeks of build time to wait for the product owner to come back from holiday.

Why this is hard

What you have just read is a longer definition of ready than the one your team probably has. That is the trade. Some teams will say it is too much. Some product owners will say it is too much. The short answer is that the cost is not really new — it is the same decision work that was being done during the build, moved to before the build. The total decision-cost is the same or smaller. What has changed is when in the week it happens.

There is a longer answer worth saying out loud, because the team will eventually say it. The reason this version of ready feels heavier is that it makes the decision debt of the work visible up front, where it used to be hidden inside the build. It used to be possible for the product owner to hand a half-formed story to the team and have the team's mid-build conversations turn it into something shippable. The team did the product owner's work, quietly, and the product owner got credit for stories that were not really fully specified when they entered the sprint. The new definition of ready ends that arrangement. The product owner has to hand something fully specified. The team's job stops being "interpret what the product owner meant" and becomes "build what the product owner actually asked for." The total amount of work in the system goes down. The visible amount of work for the product owner goes up. That second part is what the resistance is really about, and it is worth being honest about with the product owner before the resistance starts.

The conversation with the product owner

You will have a conversation with at least one product owner who tells you the new definition is "process for its own sake" or "asking for too much detail before we know what we want." Both of these are answers from the old ratio. In the old ratio, the team had run-time to figure out what was wanted. In the new ratio, what is wanted has to be figured out before the run starts.

The conversation that works, in my experience, is not the one that argues. It is the one that asks. *In the last sprint, how many of the team's stories needed a clarification mid-build that you, the product owner, had to come and answer?* Almost always, the honest answer is *most of them*. Then: *how long did each of those clarifications take, end to end, from the team's question to your answer in their hands?* Almost always: *a day or two, sometimes more*. Then: *what happens to the build if the clarification takes a day and the build itself takes four hours?* The product owner does the arithmetic in their head. The conversation has happened.

This is the same ask-don't-tell move from the one-on-ones chapter in Part 2, with the lever the new ratio has just put in your hand. You do not have to convince the product owner that the definition of ready has changed. You have to let them notice that their old habit of answering mid-build is no longer arithmetic that works.

One conversation, not three

I worked recently with a team using AI tooling at the front of its process — product manager generates the brief, business analyst writes up the stories, team picks them up. The moment that brought the dysfunction into the open was when the product manager, the business analyst, and the developers all, at about the same time, became incensed with the volume of questions flying around in testing. Each of them was watching their work get held up by other people's clarifications, and each of them privately thought the problem was with the others. The number of questions on a story, once it reached the team, had escalated very fast — far faster than it had on equivalent teams not using AI tooling.

The cause was not the tooling. The cause was that the conversation that produces a story used to be one conversation and was now three. The product manager talked to the business analyst, then the business analyst wrote up the story, then the business analyst explained it to the team, then the team asked the questions that should have been settled in the first conversation. Information travels relatively slowly between people, and serialising a single act of refinement across three people meant the same conversation had to happen three times. By the time the team picked the story up, three rounds of telephone had stripped away enough of the original intent that the team had real questions to ask, and the answers required going back up the chain.

In the old ratio the cost of this was tolerable. The build took weeks; the rounds of clarification fitted inside that. In the new ratio the rounds of clarification took longer than the build, and the team was sitting on questions while their tooling generated work they could not yet verify was correct.

The fix is the move the team's predecessors used to do without thinking about it: refinement as a team activity. Product manager, business analyst, team, in the same room or the same call, with AI tooling helping rewrite and tighten the story in real time. One conversation, every voice in it, the story emerging in front of everyone. By the end of the session the card meets the definition of ready the chapter has just described, and the team can walk away and work in parallel because the questions have already been asked and the answers are already on the card.

That move feels like a step backward — going back to the long collaborative meetings that lean methodologies told everybody to streamline ten years ago. It is not backward. It is a response to the new arithmetic. The reason team refinement felt heavy in the old ratio was that the build absorbed the cost of skipping it. The build does not absorb that cost any more. Either you pay for the refinement at the front of the work, together, or you pay for it across the sprint, separately, and at much higher cost.

Three ways it goes wrong

The first is that the team writes the new definition of ready, but treats it as advisory rather than binding. Cards still get pulled when "ready enough." The product owner is reassured that the new list is "the goal" rather than the gate. Within a sprint or two the new definition is the old definition plus more paperwork that nobody reads, and the team has the worst of both worlds — the cost of the longer list without the benefit of actually holding the line.

The second is that the new definition becomes a stick. The team uses it to push back on every story, and the relationship with the product owner turns adversarial. The point of the new definition is not to make the product owner suffer. It is to move the resolution of the decisions in the work to before the work starts, where it now belongs. A team that uses the definition of ready as a weapon ends up with a product owner who hands them maximally-specified stories that have nothing to do with what the customer actually wants. The new arrangement has to be cooperative, or it produces a different kind of dysfunction.

The third is that the team adds the new components but does not actually do the test design upfront. The card has a line saying "test plan settled" with no test plan on it. The "settled" is aspirational. The same dysfunction the chapter started with returns, in a new costume. The test plan being on the card means the team and the product owner have agreed how the work will be verified, in concrete enough terms that nobody is going to be surprised on the day the verification is supposed to happen. If the line is there but no agreement is there, the line is decoration.

The rescue

If your team's definition of ready has not changed since 2022 and your team is using AI tooling — and most teams are — you do not need a six-month process programme to update it. You need one card and an hour.

Pick the next story the team is about to start. Walk through what is going to happen to it. Write down every decision the team is going to need during the build, with the owner and the date by which it has to be answered. Write down what "good" looks like in terms two different team members would build the same thing from. Write down how the team will know it got it.

Now look at that card. If three lines that used to be implicit are now explicit, you have a new definition of ready for that one story. Run it. See what happens. If the story lands cleanly — and most of the time it will, because almost all of the apparent friction is just decisions arriving in the right order — you have the new definition for the team. If something goes wrong, you have a specific failure to learn from, on a card you can re-walk.

The new definition of ready is not bigger because process is better. It is bigger because the same decision-cost that used to be paid during the build now has to be paid before the build. The total work is the same. The order has changed. The team that does not change the order is the team whose tooling has just got four times faster and whose throughput has not. The rest of the time is going somewhere the team cannot quite name.

Chapter 18: When Testing Stopped Scaling

TESTING is where the new ratio breaks first. When code that used to take a week to build now takes an afternoon, the old arrangement — a tester picking up each card after the developer marks it done — collapses under the volume. The gate that comfortably handled one story a day is now asked to handle five. It can't, and the queue of built-but-untested work grows faster than anyone can clear it.

The constraint didn't disappear when building got fast. It moved downstream, to the next thing that couldn't speed up to match.

What manual testing used to do

The old arrangement, in most teams I have worked with, was that the bulk of the work-time on a story went into the build, and a smaller slice at the end went into testing. The tester picked up the card when the developer marked it done, clicked through the feature, looked at the obvious cases, raised any bugs they found, and signed off. If you were lucky there was an automated test suite as well, but the manual click-through was the thing that actually verified the work. It was the empirical truth. The build was thought to be correct because a person had looked at it.

If we are being honest about how this was usually staffed, the manual click-through was, in most teams, allocated to whoever was free. Often the most junior person in the room. The tester would guess what to test after the developer had built it, click a few buttons, and make a judgment. That judgment was the gate. The team's quality assurance, as actually practised, was substantially "the dumbest guy on the team guesses how to test the thing after clicking a few buttons" — and I do not mean any individual person; I mean the structural arrangement, which most teams ran by accident and the rest ran by design.

This worked, after a fashion, because the volume was tolerable. The build took most of a week; the click-through took an hour or two; whatever the click-through missed got caught in production over the following days. The system absorbed a lot of slack — decision debt about what to test, what to skip, what to defer — that was nobody's idea of robust engineering but which functioned because of the leisurely pace of the front end.

That arrangement does not survive the new ratio.

What testing has to be now

When a developer can produce four times the code in a day, and a tester cannot click four times the buttons in a day, the back gate becomes the constraint inside a week. The team has the same testing capacity it has always had. The team is now generating a multiple of the code that capacity used to be reasonable for. Something has to change, and the something is not "find more testers" — there are not more testers to find, and even if there were, the maths does not work for the next iteration of the tooling improvement either.

What has to change is what testing means at the end of the build. The work testing used to do — empirically verifying that what the developer built is what was wanted — has to be done by something that scales with code volume. Not by something that scales with human afternoons. The honest version of this, which a lot of teams have not said out loud yet, is that the empirical truth has to move from a person clicking the buttons to a comprehensive automated regression suite passing.

This is the move I have started calling the Tesla harness. It is borrowed from the manufacturing analogy, where Tesla famously uses a standardised wiring harness across products, and new product lines only have to interface with the existing harness. The infrastructure is stable. New things plug into it. The verification question is not "does this new thing work in isolation," it is "does it pass through the harness." For software the harness is the regression suite. The suite is the empirical truth. New code has to interface with it and the suite has to pass. The team's manual testing capacity is reserved for the small set of things that genuinely cannot be automated yet — visual judgment, novel user flows, anything that requires a human eye on it. Everything else is the suite's job.

What this changes about the team is not the volume of testing work — it is the location of it. The work moves from after-the-build, manually, to alongside-the-build, automatically. The tests that confirm a feature are written as the feature is written, and they run on every change going forward. The team builds up an empirical artefact that gets stronger every sprint, rather than reproducing a manual click-through every sprint.

What still has to be manual

I want to be honest about the limits of this, because the chapter is not arguing that manual testing is obsolete.

The Tesla harness is excellent at the things it can be made to verify automatically: the regression cases the team has already thought of, the boundary conditions someone has already encoded, the integration paths between known components. It is hopeless at the things it has not been told to check for. A visual regression where the layout breaks but every functional test passes will sail through the suite. A user flow that is technically correct but unusable will sail through the suite. A feature that does exactly what was specified but is the wrong feature for the customer will sail through the suite triumphantly.

The team's manual testing capacity, freed from the routine, has to spend its time on these. The new arrangement is not zero manual testing — it is manual testing reserved for what manual testing is actually good at. A few hours a week on the things the suite cannot see, rather than a tester clicking through every story to make sure it more or less does what was asked.

The test plan that goes on the card — the one chapter 17 argued has to be part of the definition of ready — is what determines this division. For each story, before the work starts, the team has agreed: this is the part the suite will verify, this is the part a person has to look at, and this is the part nobody is going to test because it is genuinely too low-risk to be worth a person's time. That third category is not a betrayal of quality. It is the team admitting honestly that testing capacity is finite and has to be spent where it matters.

Tactical batching: the move most teams have not made

Even with the Tesla harness in place, there is a tactical move on top of it that most teams have not yet made and that materially changes the testing throughput. It is to stop regressing every feature in isolation, and start regressing in batches.

The traditional rhythm is: developer finishes a story, hands it to a tester, tester runs the regression cases for that story, signs it off. Then the next story. Then the next. Each pass through the regression cases is full overhead — environment setup, context reload, the same end-to-end flows verified again. The team spends a quarter to a third of its time setting up to test rather than testing.

The batched version is: features get built and merged behind whatever flag or off-by-default state the team uses to keep production safe. The regression pass happens once, on a schedule the team can hold — once a day for fast-moving teams, once or twice a week for the rest. The regression confirms a batch of features in a single pass. The features that pass the batch release together. The features that fail the batch are isolated and fixed individually.

The difference in throughput is not subtle. The same testing capacity confirms three or four times as many features per week, because the per-feature setup overhead is amortised across the batch. For a team where testing has just become the constraint, this is often the single move that recovers the throughput AI gave them at the build.

It is not a free move. Batching means features wait longer between team-done and customer-done, because they wait for the next regression window. For teams where time-to-customer is the metric, this is a real cost. For most teams I have worked with, where time-to-customer was already days or weeks of post-done waiting, batching is a smaller wait inside a larger pipeline that was already slow. The honest accounting is per-team.

When the testers cannot keep up

I worked recently with a team where the dev side of the line had got fast and the test side had not. Testing had always taken longer than coding on this team — it had been true before AI tooling arrived. After the tooling arrived, the dev side accelerated again, and the test side stayed exactly where it was. Within a few sprints the testing column was the column with all the cards in it, and the team's flow was effectively limited by how many cards the testers could move per week.

What surprised me about the team's response was not that they struggled, which was inevitable. It was the shape of the dysfunction. The testers did not say "we cannot keep up, we need to change how we test." They started, instead, to argue about edge cases. Stories that were nominally complete and met the basic functionality of the feature were sent back to the developers in droves, with complaints about quality. The edge cases the testers were raising were not, mostly, edge cases that mattered. They were the kind of cases the team had previously agreed to defer or to accept as known limits. The complaints were not about the work. They were about the testers being overwhelmed by it and needing a way to look like they were holding the line.

This is the manual testing equivalent of the queue around the review from chapter 13. The queue was not "the work is unfinished" — the queue was "the testers cannot move work through the gate fast enough, and the dysfunction is being expressed as quality concerns to give it a respectable name." Each thing the testers raised was technically defensible. None of it was the actual problem. The actual problem was that the team's testing capacity had not scaled with its build capacity, and the testers' rational response — given that they had no other lever — was to slow down the front end with quality complaints rather than admit to being unable to keep up.

What the team should have done was a version of what this chapter has just described. Build the regression suite into the empirical truth. Reserve manual testing for what manual testing is actually for. Batch the regression passes. Agree, story by story, what level of testing each story requires before the work starts — so the testers are not making post-hoc edge-case judgments under pressure.

The team did not get there before I left. The conversation about test design upfront was had, and then it was had again, and then the next sprint started and the same defensive pattern recurred. The dysfunction outlived the intervention. Sometimes the structural fix takes longer than the engagement, and the honest accounting is that not every team you visit gets fixed. The lesson is not that the fix does not work. The lesson is that the team had built its self-image around being thorough manual testers, and surrendering that role — even to a regression suite that would have made their work easier — was a loss they were not ready to take.

Three ways it goes wrong

The first is that the team builds the regression suite but does not actually trust it. The suite passes, the team still wants a tester to look at every feature, and the suite ends up being a parallel artefact that nobody is acting on. A regression suite that does not get acted on is decoration. The team has to commit, in advance, to what the suite passing actually means — and then live with that meaning when something the suite passed turns out to have a problem in production.

The second is that the test plan on the card becomes a wish-list rather than an agreement. The card says *automated regression plus a manual pass plus a stakeholder check*, and what actually happens is the automated regression, because by the time the manual pass and the stakeholder check are due the team has moved on to the next story. Three lines on the card with no enforcement is exactly the same dysfunction the last chapter warned about. The test plan is real or it is decoration.

The third is over-automating the things that genuinely need a human, and under-automating the things that genuinely need a machine. Visual layout, novel user experience, the question of whether the customer actually wants this — these need a person, and the team that tries to put them in the suite produces brittle tests nobody trusts. Routine integration, regression of known flows, boundary conditions — these need a machine, and the team that keeps doing them manually produces tester burnout and an inevitable miss. The split has to be deliberate, and the test plan on each card is where it gets named.

The rescue

If your team's testing column is the column where all the cards live, and the testers' complaints about quality are arriving faster than the team can address them, you do not need a better tester. You need to change what testing means at the end of your build.

Three moves, none of which require a budget. Audit the regression suite the team already has — most teams have one and have not looked at it in a year — and identify what it actually covers. Then for the next three stories, agree the test plan on the card before the work starts: what the suite verifies, what a person needs to look at, and what is honestly out of scope. Run those three stories through that arrangement and see what happens. If the cards move and nothing bad reaches production, you have your evidence that the team's old testing model was carrying weight it did not need to. If something does reach production, you have a specific failure to learn from and a specific gap to close in the suite.

Test capacity is finite, and AI did not change that. The volume of new code arriving at the test gate is no longer finite in the same way. The team that does not change how testing works is the team whose testers will tell you, with technical justification and visible exhaustion, that they cannot keep up. The team is right about the symptom and wrong about the cause. The cause is that the gate they are guarding is not the gate the work needs any more.

Chapter 19: When Defining Becomes the Job

THE front of the board is now the constraint — and the front of the board is not the team.

For three parts of this book, the person who decides what the team should build has been an input to the team's work: someone who hands over requirements, answers questions, sets direction. An input you managed, but not the bottleneck. That has changed. When the team can build almost as fast as it can be told what to build, the speed of the telling becomes the limit. Whoever defines the work is now the slowest step in the system — which makes defining the work the job that matters most, and the one nobody has been treating as the constraint.

The pattern from chapter 1, revisited

Chapter 1 listed five patterns the diagnosis turns up. One of them was the sign-off chokepoint — work waiting on a single overloaded person. Another was the escalation reflex — a team that has lost the habit of deciding and routes every choice upward. Both were, in chapter 1, problems the rest of the book promised to address with cheap fixes.

The cheap fixes in Part 3 attacked the chokepoint side of these. Chapter 13's cycle-time exercise surfaces the column where work waits. Chapter 15's graveyard exercise retires decisions the team is not going to make. The escalation reflex side was harder, because the cheap fixes the book had to offer the team did not necessarily reach the people above the team — and the team's escalations went to those people.

In the old ratio that was a tolerable limitation. The team could be improved, the team's flow could be improved, and the cost of the upstream escalation problem was absorbed by everything else that was slow. In the new ratio it is not absorbed by anything. When the build takes hours, the time the team spends waiting for an upstream decision is no longer a sliver of the sprint. It is the sprint.

The product owner who escalates rather than deciding, the product manager who is too busy with their day job to engage with the team, the head of product who has not made a roadmap call in six weeks — all of these were always part of why teams went slowly. They were never the only part. They are now disproportionately the part.

What product functions used to do

The arrangement that worked, for most of the time I have been in this profession, was a kind of cooperative interpolation. The product person had ideas about what should be built and a rough sense of what mattered. The team had time inside the build to work out the details. Between them, slowly, over the course of a sprint, what was actually wanted emerged. The product person did not need to be precise because the team filled in the precision. The team did not need to ask too many questions because the product person was around enough to answer the urgent ones.

What that meant in practice is that the product function was carried by the team. The team did a lot of the work that, in a stricter accounting, would have been called product work — deciding which edge cases mattered, which trade-offs were acceptable, which behaviour to ship by default. The product person signed off on these decisions but the team made them. That arrangement carried real decision debt; the new ratio just stopped letting the build absorb it.

The build absorbed the cost of that arrangement, in the same way it absorbed everything else. When the build takes six weeks, the team has time inside it to make a hundred small product decisions and have them all be reasonable. When the build takes six hours, the team does not have that time. The product function has to actually function — has to produce, in advance, the decisions the team used to make for it during the build.

The change of expectation here is not subtle, and not many product organisations have noticed it yet. The product person whose job used to be "give the team something to work on" now has a job which is closer to "have decided what the team is building, in enough detail that the team can build it without further input." Those two jobs sound similar. They are different jobs, and the second one is meaningfully harder.

When AI is asked to do the job for them

The honest thing to say next is that a lot of product organisations have responded to the new pressure not by doing the harder job, but by using AI tooling to manufacture the appearance of having done it.

I worked recently with a team where the instruction had come down from management that everyone should be writing stories with AI. Product managers would type a two-sentence brief into the tooling and press the button; the tooling generated an epic and a set of requirements. Business analysts were instructed to take that output and pump it through their own AI prompts to generate the detailed acceptance criteria. The team then picked up the result and tried to build it.

The product managers, when I talked to them, often had no idea what they wanted built. Not in the lazy sense — in the structural sense. They had not spoken to a customer in months. They had no concrete picture of what the feature was supposed to do or what would make it good. Under pressure from management to keep the team supplied with stories, they pressed the button and hoped. The business analysts, downstream, did the same. The acceptance criteria that arrived at the team's board were long, formally correct, and substantively empty.

The team's developers used AI tooling to decipher the requirements that AI tooling had generated. They complained, often, about how verbose the stories were. The work that came out of this pipeline was sometimes what the customer wanted and more often was not — but the team had been told the stories were "ready" and was building what the page said.

The most efficient feature factory I have seen in twenty years. Stories generated in tens and hundreds, in isolation from team and customer, all of them formally satisfying the criteria the team had been told to hold. None of them, as far as anyone could tell, settled the question of what the customer was actually being given. The team had drifted so far away from the source — the customer, the actual problem the work was meant to solve — under the guise of productivity that it was unbelievable.

The lesson is not that the team should not have used AI. The product managers should have. The team should have. The lesson is that AI tooling can manufacture the appearance of having decided without any of the underlying work having been done. It can produce documents that look exactly like the output of a product function that knows what it wants, generated by a product function that does not. The constraint hides behind the productivity theatre, and the team cannot see it from where they are sitting, because the cards keep arriving.

What product has to look like now

What the team needs from a functioning product owner in the new ratio is not more stories per week. It is fewer stories, each one of which represents an actual decision that an actual person has actually made about an actual customer's actual problem.

What that looks like in practice is a product function that is closer to the customer than it has been in years. Closer enough that the answers to the questions the team will ask are already in the product owner's head before the team asks them, because the product owner has just been with the people the work is for. Closer enough that the demo or the wireframe or the working prototype the product owner brings to refinement is grounded in something real, not generated from a prompt. Closer enough that the product owner can defend, in front of the team, why this work and not the next work — and the defence is in terms of customer outcomes the product owner has heard about directly.

This is not a methodology. It is a return to what the role used to be when it functioned, plus a recognition that the role can no longer be done at arm's length from the customer. The product owner who is a coordinator between stakeholders and the team is a role that the new ratio has retired. The product owner who is the customer's representative inside the team, with the customer's problems and language and preferences alive in their head, is the role that has just become essential.

There is an empirical test the chapter can offer here, and it is worth asking out loud the next time you are unsure whether your product function is keeping up. Can your product owner, your product manager, your business analyst — can any of them tell you, without their tooling, what the customer asked for, which customer asked for it, and why this work was prioritised over the next thing on the list? If they can, you are in good hands. If they cannot, the cards arriving at your board are slop dressed up as readiness, and no amount of acceptance-criteria sophistication is going to save the team downstream.

The conversation with the people above the team

The chapter has to be honest that the fix here is not entirely available to the delivery manager.

The product function reports up through a different chain than the team does. The director of product, the VP of product, the customer team, the sales organisation — none of these answer to you, and many of the levers that would change how product is being done are theirs. What you can do, and have to do, is name the constraint to the people who can move on it.

The conversation that tends to land, in my experience, is not the one that complains. It is the one that does the arithmetic. *Here is the throughput the team is now capable of. Here is the throughput we are actually achieving. Here is the difference, and here is where the time is going.* When the difference is largely "the team is waiting for product decisions" — and after the work of Parts 3 and 4 it usually is — the conversation about whose problem that is happens on its own.

You should not expect to win this conversation the first time. Senior product people, like senior anyone, do not respond well to being told their function is the constraint. They will respond, often, by pushing the work back onto the team — *the team should be writing better stories themselves*, or *the team should be more autonomous about deciding what to build.* Both of these are exactly the kind of carrying that the old ratio used to absorb and the new one cannot. The conversation has to keep returning to the arithmetic. The team can deliver what is decided. The team cannot decide what to deliver. That is the product function's job, and the new ratio has made it a full one.

Three ways it goes wrong

The first is that the team starts deciding what to build itself, in the absence of a functioning product function. This sometimes looks fine for a sprint or two. The team is technical, the team is close to the work, the team has opinions about what should be done. What the team is not is the customer, and over time the work the team chooses drifts away from what the customer needs. The delivery manager who lets this happen has substituted one set of constraint-hiding for another. The right move is to keep pushing the conversation upstream, not to fill the gap.

The second is that the new product function gets defined as "write more detail" rather than "decide more clearly." A product organisation that responds to the pressure by producing fifty-page specifications has not understood the problem. Detail without grounding is exactly what the slop pipeline produces. The deliverable from a working product function is decisions — about scope, about priority, about what success looks like — not pages.

The third is that the team stops asking the questions because the answers never come back useful. This is the worst of the failure modes. A team that has learned not to ask is a team that has accepted whatever shows up on the board, and the feedback loop between the work and what the work is for breaks. The delivery manager's job, when this is happening, is to keep the questions alive — to make the team's questions visible to the people who should be answering them, even when those people are not answering. The cost of letting the team go quiet is paid in everything the team builds afterwards.

The rescue

If your team is using AI tooling and shipping more code per sprint than it has ever shipped, and the customer's experience of the team's work is not getting better at the same rate, the bottleneck is probably no longer inside the team.

The team has done what it can do. The cycle time is short. The board is honest. The definition of ready is bulletproof. The testing capacity is matched to the volume. And still, somehow, what gets shipped is not landing for the customer. What is happening is that the cards arriving at the team's board are decisions that have not been made — wishes dressed up as specifications — and no amount of downstream excellence is going to convert wishes into a product the customer needs.

The move, in that case, is not another exercise inside the team. It is the conversation with the product function that names what is happening. You will need the arithmetic. You will need the team's numbers, the team's throughput, the gap between what the team can deliver and what is actually being shipped. You will need the patience to have the conversation more than once. And you will need to be willing to say, plainly, to people more senior than you, that the work above the team is not keeping up.

This is the part of the delivery manager's job that the title actually pays for. Not the standup, not the retro, not the exercises in Part 3. The conversation with the people who can move the constraint above the team is where the new ratio puts the biggest gain. The cost of having that conversation is the cost of admitting that the problem is harder than the team having a process problem. The cost of not having it is everything the team builds drifting further from what the customer needs, while everyone above the team congratulates themselves on the velocity.

The book began with five patterns of a system that no longer works for the people inside it. It is ending with the recognition that the same patterns, in the new ratio, have just got bigger and more expensive. The bottleneck has been the same all along. AI did not change what it is. It made it impossible to keep ignoring. The work in front of you, if you are still reading, is the work the book has been pointing at the whole time.

Conclusion

THE teams that fix themselves do not do it by buying better tools, hiring more consultants, or adopting a new framework. They do it by learning to see — seeing the constraint, seeing the decision debt, seeing the difference between a ceremony and a ritual.

Light touch is not a methodology. It is a discipline. It is the refusal to substitute motion for progress. It is the willingness to make the smallest move that produces the largest change, even when a larger move would feel more decisive. It is the habit of asking why before asking how, and of trusting your team to find the answer once the right question is on the table.

The fixes in this book are cheap because the real work is not in the fix. It is in the diagnosis. A team that knows where its decisions are stuck can unblock itself with a conversation. A team that does not know will spend a year and a budget on a transformation that touches nothing load-bearing.

Your job as a delivery manager is not to have all the answers. It is to see the system clearly enough to know where the next question goes. Do that consistently, and the team will do the rest. The constraint is rarely code. It is rarely budget. It is almost always a decision that has been waiting too long to be made.

Make it.

Afterword

BY now you have seen the diagnosis, the ceremonies, and the cheap fixes. You have the vocabulary — decision debt, intentional work, the open mode, the volunteer model. You have the lens: look for the constraint, not the complaint.

What you do with it is up to you.

Some readers will put this book down and go back to their teams unchanged. The ceremonies will stay the same. The board will stay the same. The decisions will stay queued behind the same overloaded person, and six months from now the retro will surface the same five complaints. Nothing in this book can stop that. Only you can.

Other readers will see one thing — just one — that they can change tomorrow. A standup that walks the board right to left and actually produces a decision. A work-in-progress limit that forces the team to finish before it starts. A clarification asked at the standup instead of escalated to a manager who does not have the context. One light move. One unblocked loop. One week where work moves faster than it did the week before.

That is the whole game. Not the transformation programme. Not the framework rollout. One light move, observed, owned, and repeated, until a team that could not get anything finished is quietly getting everything finished, and nobody can point to the single day it changed.

The teams that get better do not get better all at once. They get better one decision at a time.

Yours is the next one.

Before You Go

YOU'VE got the lens now, and the levers. The rest is doing it — one light move at a time, on the team in front of you, this week.

Most readers will close the book here and get on with exactly that. That's the right outcome, and it's the whole point of the book.

This last part is for two people in particular.

The first is whoever is accountable for a delivery organisation that has quietly stopped being predictable. Your teams ship more than they ever have. The roadmap still slips, the dates still surprise you, and when the board asks why, the honest answer is harder to give than it should be. You've funded the tooling, run the reorganisations, paid for the certifications — and the work still waits. I fix that, and what it almost always comes down to is the thing this book is about: decisions queuing where nobody can see them. I take on a small number of organisations and the leaders who run them. The conversation starts at the site below.

The second is the person inside one of those teams who recognised it on every page — the delivery manager, the engineering manager, the one who already knows where the work is stuck and just wants it to stop. For you I've put the **first-week diagnostic** on the site: the actual questions I run over a delivery org before I change anything. It's free. Run your own teams against it, and you'll have a real shortlist by the end of the day — the kind of thing worth putting in front of whoever holds the budget. Leave an email and I'll send it across, with the occasional note when I write something worth your time.

rowangobey.com

Find the constraint. Make the lightest move. Get out of the way.

That's the job. Now go and do it.

Acknowledgements

This book would not exist without the people who taught me, challenged me, and occasionally rescued me from my own bad ideas.

To Craig — who saw potential in me before I saw it in myself. He put me in front of clients, gave me access to rooms I had no right to be in, and threw me in the deep end knowing I would come back fighting. Without his support, his trust, and his willingness to open doors, none of the work this book describes would have been possible. I hope it makes him proud.

To Daamon — my first coach, and the person who pushed me to develop when I was still figuring out whether I had anything worth developing. He did not let me settle. Everything that came after started with him.

To the teams who let me in: You know who you are. The standups that ran long, the retros that went sideways, the planning sessions where nobody agreed on what we were building — every one of them taught me something I could not have learned from a book. Thank you for trusting me with your dysfunctions. I hope I repaid some of that trust.

To the colleagues who became friends: For the conversations in airport lounges, Slack threads at midnight, and the occasional necessary pint after a difficult week. For reading early drafts and telling me when something was nonsense. For not letting me get away with "that'll do."

To the clients who took a chance: Especially the ones who hired me when I was unproven, and then hired me again. There is no better validation than a second engagement.

To Echo, Violet, and George: Again. For everything.

To Sasa: For your enduring friendship, support and helping to keep me sane.

To Dad, Mom, and Laura: For getting me here.

About the Author

Rowan Gobey is a delivery management consultant who helps software teams move faster by changing less.

Across more than fifteen years in and around technology — as a management consultant, in logistics and operations roles where he was the customer of engineering teams, and for the past several years inside delivery management itself — Rowan has learned the same lesson from every angle: the thing slowing a team down is almost never the code. His approach is simple. Find the constraint, make the lightest move that unblocks it, and get out of the way before the team forgets it was ever stuck. Not an agile coach with a certificate — a practitioner who has sat in the standups, read the boards, and fixed the bottlenecks everyone else was too busy to see.

Rowan uses the idea of **decision debt** — the hidden cost of queued, deferred, and escalated decisions — to explain the real reason most software teams slow down long before their code quality does. It is the idea this book is built on.

He writes on systems thinking, team dynamics, and software delivery. He lives in Melbourne with his family and an unreasonable number of whiteboards.

Learn more at rowangobey.com

Further Reading

THE thinking in this book stands on the shoulders of several writers and practitioners who saw the same problems from different angles. If you want to go deeper, start here.

On constraints and systems thinking

- *The Goal* — Eliyahu M. Goldratt and Jeff Cox (1984). The book that started it all. A novel about a factory manager who learns that optimising anything except the bottleneck is just making the warehouse fuller. The translation to software is direct.
- *Critical Chain* — Eliyahu M. Goldratt (1997). Applies constraint theory to project management. Essential reading if your team's projects are always late despite everyone being busy.
- *Thinking in Systems* — Donella H. Meadows (2008). The clearest introduction to systems thinking ever written. Read the chapter on leverage points twice.

On software delivery and DevOps

- *The Phoenix Project* — Gene Kim, Kevin Behr, and George Spafford (2013). The novel that made DevOps comprehensible to executives. If you need to explain why IT matters to a board, give them this.
- *Accelerate* — Nicole Forsgren, Jez Humble, and Gene Kim (2018). The research-backed case for why delivery performance predicts organisational performance. The metrics in this book are the ones you should be tracking.

- *Team Topologies* — Matthew Skelton and Manuel Pais (2019). How to design teams around the flow of work rather than the org chart. The inverse Conway manoeuvre is one of the most powerful ideas in modern software organisation.
- *Continuous Delivery* — Jez Humble and David Farley (2010). The technical companion to this book. If your deployment pipeline is the constraint, read this next.

On teams, culture, and management

- *Peopleware* — Tom DeMarco and Timothy Lister (1987, updated 2013). The classic on why software projects fail for human reasons, not technical ones. Still relevant thirty years later.
- *The Manager's Path* — Camille Fournier (2017). The best practical guide to engineering management. Read it after you have fixed your team's flow and need to know what good management looks like day to day.
- *An Elegant Puzzle* — Will Larson (2019). Systems of engineering management. Larson thinks in systems the way this book thinks in constraints.
- *Turn the Ship Around!* — L. David Marquet (2012). Intent-based leadership and the shift from telling to asking. The volunteer model in this book owes a debt to Marquet's thinking.

On lean, flow, and the Toyota Production System

- *The Toyota Production System* — Taiichi Ohno (1988). The original. Dense, but worth it for the clarity of Ohno's thinking about waste, flow, and the Andon cord.

- *Lean Software Development* — Mary and Tom Poppendieck (2003). Translates lean manufacturing principles to software with remarkable fidelity.

On writing and thinking clearly

- *The Elements of Style* — William Strunk Jr. and E.B. White (1918/1959). Because a team that cannot describe its problem clearly cannot solve it.

If you have a book that should be on this list, let me know. I am always looking for the next clear explanation of a muddy problem.

Glossary

Decision debt. The accumulation of decisions that have been deferred, queued, or routed to someone who hasn't made them yet. Work waiting on a decision rather than on more work. Like technical debt, it accrues quietly and is paid for later, usually in cycle time. The central concept of this book: most delivery slowness is decision debt, and AI compressing build time has made it the dominant cost rather than a minor one.

The ceremonies. The recurring events of a team's working week — the one-on-one, the standup, planning, refinement, the retro, the demo, estimation, and the spike. This book treats each as a feedback loop: a point where information goes in and a decision comes out. A ceremony that produces no decision is a meeting, not a feedback loop.

Feedback loop. A point in a team's work where information is taken in, a decision is made, and the work moves on as a result. The unit this book uses to judge whether a ceremony is doing its job. Frameworks specify that the loops exist; they don't supply the thinking that makes them worth running.

Intentional work. Work picked up deliberately rather than by reflex — with a clear picture of what it is, what it is not, and what would tell you it is finished. The opposite is not laziness but sleepwalking: moving through the ceremonies competently and on time without ever quite deciding anything.

Work-time vs elapsed-time. Work-time is how long a piece of work actually takes to do. Elapsed-time is how long it sits on the board from start to finish, including all the waiting. The two are usually wildly different — a three-day task can spend nineteen days on the board — and confusing them is why teams commit to more than their process can deliver. Commitments made in work-time and lived in elapsed-time don't hold.

Cycle time. The total elapsed time from when a card enters the board to when it leaves — work plus waiting. Most of it, for most teams, is waiting.

Spike. A time-boxed investigation whose only product is a decision, or enough information for someone to make one. A spike does not build the thing; it produces the specific knowledge a blocked decision is waiting on. A spike that ends in more code instead of a decision has missed its job.

Discovery. A deliberately bounded body of investigation — a planned set of spikes with one overall goal, one timebox, and one decision point at the end. What a team reaches for when a single question has unravelled into a whole territory of them.

Definition of ready. The bar a card has to clear before it can be pulled into progress — a short, concrete list of what must be true for the team to start. In the new ratio, the bar moves from "we know enough to start" to "we know enough to finish," because there is no longer enough build-time to absorb an unresolved question.

Definition of done. The short list of conditions a team will genuinely refuse to move a card past until they are true. The honest version is the longest version of done the team can actually commit to and hold — not the customer's done, which usually sits past the team's control.

Velocity. How much work a team actually completes per sprint, used for forecasting. A useful internal planning input; a corrosive external productivity metric. Velocity already contains all of a team's waiting time, which is why it forecasts more honestly than adding up work-time estimates.

Forecast (vs estimate). An estimate is a point prediction ("three weeks"). A forecast is a range with explicit assumptions ("between weeks four and seven, assuming the platform team ships by Wednesday"). The book argues for forecasts: they're honest about uncertainty, they name the assumptions that can be challenged, and they put the team in a defensible position when an assumption breaks.

The open mode (open by default). The operating rule that process work happens visibly — the team can see what's being worked on, who's leading it, and where it stands. Distinguished from closed-door managerial work (performance, hiring, restructures), which stays private. The failure mode to avoid is the half-measure: hinting at quiet work rather than being either open or silent.

The volunteer model. Asking the team for a volunteer to lead an improvement, rather than assigning one. Self-selected ownership predicts completion far better than assignment, and it signals that the team's improvements are theirs to drive. To lead is to ensure the work happens — not necessarily to do it.

Benevolent dictator (mode). A temporary mode for a team that has stopped believing improvement is possible, where the delivery manager drives the first one or two improvements personally to prove change is achievable, then hands the mechanism back to the volunteer model. Borrowed from open-source governance. Used to bootstrap trust, then abandoned.

Light touch. The operating principle of Part 1: the lightest move that produces the largest change. The effort goes into finding the one lever that moves the work, not into pulling many. A heavy touch — a transformation programme, a framework rollout — is usually a failure to understand which lever actually matters.

Kaizen. From the Toyota Production System: continuous improvement made of small, regular changes rather than occasional large ones. The premise behind the retro — one improvement per cycle, compounding across a year, beats waiting for a single big transformation.

The impact-by-effort matrix. The 2x2 grid (impact on one axis, effort on the other) the team uses to surface and rank what's worth acting on. The high-impact, low-effort quadrant is the fix list. The argument that happens while placing items is more valuable than the finished grid.

The Tesla harness. The move, in the testing chapter, of making a comprehensive automated regression suite the empirical truth that new code must pass through, rather than relying on a person to click through every change. Borrowed from manufacturing: stable infrastructure that new work plugs into. Reserves scarce manual testing for what only a human eye can judge.

The new ratio. The shift, central to Part 4, in the proportion of delivery time spent building versus deciding. When building took weeks, decision debt was a sliver of the timeline; when building takes hours, decision debt is most of it. AI didn't create the bottleneck — it changed the ratio enough that the bottleneck became impossible to ignore.

www.ingramcontent.com/pod-product-compliance
Lightning Source LLC
LaVergne TN
LVHW090312210926
848480LV00001B/220
9781764734707